MW00476539

E

"Jeff Kemp has been a leader of men his entire adult life. From star quarterback to inspirational life leader. He now provides us a game plan based on following the way of the ultimate man at the center of history and the Bible."

Jim Nantz—CBS Sports Commentator

"Recently, I've been struggling with Jesus and the NFL in a love-hate relationship. I quit watching the last two seasons. I wondered if I was too biased to find anything worthwhile to say about this book. Instead, I burned through it, enjoying almost every page. Football, manhood, life, love and some of the greatest NFL stories you never heard packed in a compact resource that every man and every fan should read. Jeff Kemp has figured out the play that each of us men must receive to be all Christ called us to be. This book has stories you need, truth you can live by, and practical, easy-to-execute advice that will give you years of value. It will energize your small group. It made me start retooling my definition of what it means to be a good friend. Jeff's range of experiences, transparency about his failures, and insights will help every man become a better father, husband, friend, and son who is closer to God and better equipped for Kingdom impact. If you like football and great stories like the 'sound of silence' story, and if you like Jesus, this will be one of the best reads of your life. If you only like any two of those three, this book will still make your top ten."

C. Jeffrey Wright—CEO, Urban Ministries, Inc. (UMI)

"Every man who reads this book will be stunned at how simple, yet profound, it is from the very beginning. It is as practical as it is deep."

Patrick Lencioni—Best-selling author of *The Five Dysfunctions of a Team* and *The Six Types of Working Genius*

"*Receive* is timely encouragement for all men and excellent help to become who they are meant to be by turning to our Lord as your most relevant role model. I strongly encourage all men to read this book We will all benefit from grasping what it is to receive The Way of Jesus, instead of performing for it or pretending."

Michael W. Smith—Multi-platinum singer, songwriter, and author

"Great stories, super practical, but also richly insightful and deeply transformational. I think men are going to love this book!"

John Eldredge—Author of *Wild at Heart*

"*Receive* will help men know who they are and why they're alive. It's practical, relevant, and simple. Every man can understand the message and apply it because it depends on God, not us. I appreciate how Jeff reminds men that we must receive our identity, not try to earn it. This book will guide men to do just that."

Dr. Tony Evans—President, The Urban Alternative
and Senior Pastor, *Oak Cliff Bible Fellowship*

"I've studied lots of men in my research. One common thread is that when someone believes in them, men want to live up to that belief. My friend Jeff Kemp believes in men. He shares how our Father believes in and equips men to see a new identity for themselves and to live to a higher standard than our culture expects. *Receive* shows men how to get there. I'm excited for my college age son to capture this vision when I give him this book."

Shaunti Feldhahn—Best-selling author of *For
Women Only* and *For Men Only*

"Since we were together in the NFL decades ago, Jeff and I have been committed to sharing God's way to hope and unity. *Receive* has a radical solution for men that comes from the WAY OF JESUS. Men, this book gives you honesty, vision, and the hope of God's power to live your God-given identity. Experience this book with your buddies. Transformation and a life of impact is around the corner."

Pastor Miles McPherson—The Rock Church San
Diego, author of *The Third Option*

"*Receive* is the perfect book to equip you, challenge you, and inspire you to become the man you want to be—sold out to God, faithful to your calling, and a blessing to your family. Well-written, hard-hitting, but encouraging, Jeff Kemp has created a wonderful resource for individual men or small groups seeking to explore what matters most as men."

Gary Thomas—Author of *Sacred Marriage* and Teaching
Pastor, Cherry Hills Community Church

"Benjamin Franklin said at the start of the Revolutionary War, 'We must hang together, or we will hang separately.' How true that was for building our new nation. And how much more true that is in building a new life as a man in Jesus. We need teammates. We need the help of others! And in *Receive*, Jeff Kemp offers us a path in how best to come spiritually alive by coming together."

Robert Lewis—Founder of BetterMan and
Author of *Raising a Modern Day Knight*

"I've known Jeff Kemp for more than 25 years. He's the real deal. He connects with any man and brings passion to walking the way of Jesus. That's why I didn't have to think twice about endorsing this important book. Let's face it, you can't earn God's love. It's an impossibility. You can only receive it as a grace gift. Allow *Receive* to guide you as you become the man God designed us to be."

Les Parrott, Ph.D.—#1 New York Times
bestselling author of *Love Like That*

"*Receive* guides you in practical ways to grow out of insecurity, approval seeking, and performing out of a false self into freedom and purpose living out of your true identity as a son of God. This book will give you the spiritual and actionable resources to process your life personally and with real friends."

David Robbins—President & CEO, FamilyLife

"Identity, integrity, and influence; show me a man who knows who he is in Christ, walks with integrity and exerts biblically substantiated influence and I will show a man who is receiving from Father God and changing the world! This is why Jeff Kemp wrote this book. It's not just a must read, it's a must do!"

Samuel Rodriguez—President/CEO, National Hispanic Christian
Leadership Coalition and Author of *Your Mess, God's Miracle!*

"Jeff calls some plays that can liberate and truly set men free to experience life at a new level—fully alive, fully free. Too many suffer losing at the game of life or playing the wrong game altogether. Jeff courageously calls men up with practical truth, plays and vision that can change legacies for generations to come."

Mike Sharrow—CEO, C12 Business Forums

"Jeff Kemp is unapologetic! He knows that your identity will command your energy. It will either help or harm those connected to you. The lie today is to abandon a strong identity in God, try to earn it or simply retreat under the blitz of cultural pressure. The truth is that when you live out your truest identity—like Jesus did—you fulfill your destiny and bless many. With this book in your hands, you'll be strong for others and dangerous for good."

Kenny Luck—Founder and CEO of Every Man
Ministries and Author of *Dangerous Good*

"Jeff Kemp gained some pressure-tested insights on life, authenticity, and manhood during his NFL career. Insecurity blitzed him every week and season, despite his desires for an impressive image for the world. Jeff shares how his failures—and those of his fellow athletes—taught him the power of humility, teamwork, respect, and forgiveness. If you're tired of striving to make a name for yourself, let this book inspire you to receive and live from your true identity in Christ."

Dr. Greg Smalley—Vice President of Marriage, Focus on the Family and author of *Reconnected*

"Time and again in marriage counseling, I've seen relationships and families shatter when husbands become isolated and disconnected. In *Receive*, Jeff Kemp helps men avoid isolation by building connection, friendships, and accountability. Women, this book will encourage and inspire the men in your life. It reminds them to find their strength and identity in Jesus Christ."

Erin Smalley, BSN, MS, LPC—Smalley Marriage and Individual Counseling

"Jeff Kemp's latest book, *Receive*, is a masterfully written playbook to help every man live out his story, love his wife, and leave a legacy of blessing to his children for generations to come. Jeff was a gutsy quarterback in the NFL and has now thrown the ultimate pass to every man. You'll learn how to receive everything you need from Father God to be the man, husband, father, and friend you have always wanted to be."

Ed Tandy McGlasson—Author, Life Coach, and Founder of Blessing of the Father Ministries

"I've met very few guys who take their role as a disciple more seriously than Jeff Kemp. If you're trying your best to follow Jesus and become the man God is calling you to be, you need to read this book."

Jerrad Lopes—Founder of the *Dad Tired Podcast*

"This book is for champions in the making . . . men who want more in life. Men who want to be all that God designed them to be. It's for the guy who's confused, struggling, in a rut or just wants to be a better man. Dig in and recruit some other guys to join you on this journey."

Mark Merrill—President, Family First and All Pro Dad

"In the 1970's it was, 'I don't need a man.' In the 1990's it became, 'I don't *want* a man.' Today, it's, "What *is* a man?' Most men walk around in a masculinity-fog, looking for answers in all the wrong places, forging a trail of broken relationships and chaos. Jeff lays out a clear vision for manhood, calling men to the ancient paths. A compass, light, and guide—men need this book."

Chris Harper—Chief Storyteller & CEO, BetterMan

"Jeff Kemp's new book, *Receive*, is a refreshing and easy read. It's uplifting because Jeff writes with vulnerability. It's rare that a man of Jeff's stature would disclose more of his challenges in life than victories. Vulnerability is too rare and I commend Jeff for opening his heart in a transparent way that shows how it will help you. *Receive* will be a valuable guide for any man, or small group, who is serious about living an authentic life."

Ken Canfield, PhD—Founder, National Center for Fathering

"*Receive* is as timely as it is practical. Its message of manhood rooted in the humility and strength of Jesus is vital, as our country battles a decades-long crisis of father absence. Children need their dads and dads need to be strengthened with this clarion call for men to work together to raise each other up, to sharpen our collective iron. Fathers and future fathers who receive this message prove that being a good father comes from being a good man first. I pray that dads and young men grab this book, ask its important questions, and take the practical actions at the end of every chapter!"

Christopher A. Brown, M.A.—President, National Fatherhood Initiative

"Every man I know would benefit from the message of this book. I love how Jeff Kemp weaves his personal story as an NFL quarterback and follower of Christ in this compelling game plan for life. Men, 'he gets us.'"

Jim Burns, PhD—President, HomeWord, Author of *Doing Life with Your Adult Children: Keep Your Mouth Shut and the Welcome Mat Out*

"When we build godly men, everyone wins! It's true and Jeff Kemp knows it. That is why he wrote this book—for everybody. The adjustments that good men make as a result of reading and processing this book will impact generations."

Brian Doyle—Founder, Iron Sharpens Iron

"For years, I struggled with my identity. Wounds from all of the words spoken over me, before meeting the Lord Jesus, were my only 'truth'. After meeting the Lord, the truth of the word of God revealed that much of what I believed about myself was a lie. *Receive* is a fantastic weapon to combat the lies that the enemy has sown into the hearts of every man. Jeff has done an amazing job equipping men like me with the tools needed to truly receive everything that God has for each of us. Every guy needs this book in their arsenal. It's a game changer."

David Dusek—Founder and Executive Director, Rough Cut Men Ministries

"Every man on earth would benefit from reading *Receive*. In this book, Jeff Kemp tackles one of the biggest temptations men face: finding their identity from something other than what God says about them. Stop clawing and striving to become someone. Instead, rest in the peace and identity your heavenly father wants to give you! Read this book now."

Kent Evans—Executive Director of Manhood
Journey and Author of *Bring Your Hammer*

"For too long, a man's identity has been based on what he does, who he knows or what he owns and as a result it has left men driftless, and always searching for something more. In his new book, *Receive*, Jeff Kemp takes us back to the only real model of manhood, Jesus and helps us discover where our true identity is found."

Steve Sonderman—Founder and Executive
Director of No Regrets Men's Ministry

"Jeff Kemp addresses a crucial need in our world today—Biblical Manhood. Since men have increasingly worked away from their home and family, there has been a deadly decline in men's relevance in their family, neighborhood, workplace, and local church. Too many men have surrendered their identity as a believer and God-given responsibility for their family. The result is weakened faith in men and their families. Fatherlessness has become a devastating plague in our world.

I love Jeff's reminder, "You don't have to earn your identity or prove your manhood. Your identity is received, not achieved." He's on point that everything good in our life has happened because of what we have received from God—beginning with our identity. Becoming our best selves comes when we realize it's not about us and our abilities but being connected to and receiving from our Heavenly Father. Everything can change when a man allows God to work through him. A humble, surrendered life, firmly connected to a few friends who love and support us will receive from God and give to others. Jeff helps us walk on this journey—and be transformed!"

Dr. Jim Grassi, Founder & Rev. Wendell A. Morton,
Executive Director, Men's Ministry Catalyst

"I know no man more qualified to help you discover the value of a Men's Huddle than Jeff Kemp. Jeff knows how essential the huddle is. *Receive* brings manhood from Jesus and friendship in your huddle to life. When you get your identity and calling as a man from God, He will equip and align you with Jesus and the Father to fulfill your unique calling and responsibilities. Soak up the truths of this book, huddle up and receive the life God has for you."

Rod Handley—Founder & President, Character that Counts

"I believe this book will be a giant leap forward for the man who is ready to take a strategic and transformational step on his journey to be the man God has created him to be."

Bob Lepine—Former co-host, *FamilyLife Today*
and author, *Love Like You Mean It*

"At a time of confusion over the most basic principles of life from God our Father, Jeff Kemp gives us the perfect guide to gain our real identity and purpose. If you want a clear vision of a Godly man and practical steps to live in God's design for your life, you owe it to yourself and those you love to immerse yourself in this amazing book. Thank you, Jeff, for faithfully bringing God's message for such a time in *Receive*."

Clair Hoover—Executive Director, National Coalition of Ministries to Men

"After reading *Receive*, I came to understand my own insecurity from growing up without a father after my folks separated when I was nine. Jeff decodes the common insecurity in men and gives answers that build a solid core. This book covers all the bases on what causes men to fail. It actually shows how we can follow Jesus as our role model for building strong relationships with God the Father, friends and our loved ones. *Receive* would be great for friends or a group of men to read together, discuss, and disarm their insecurities. It offers a platform for us to build each other up and become stronger men and fathers. I'm grateful to Jeff for writing this book, and I'm excited to share it with my friends from the Durano Father School of USA."

Peter Hwang—Director of English Ministry
at Durano Father School of USA

"Jeff Kemp's passion for God, men, and what God can accomplish in a man's life is evident in his book *Receive*. Through impactful stories and his own vulnerable sharing, Jeff helps us see a plan, purpose, and God-inspired relational process for what each man can become. This book for young and old alike will help each reader develop a strong, confident, and more capable identity as they lead wherever they serve."

Roy Smith, MDiv, PhD—Founder, LiveUp Resources
and Author of *Knights of the 21st Century*

"I am so thankful that Jeff has written this 'playbook' on manhood and fatherhood because we are inundated with so much information—we don't need just another book. However, Jeff has captured the foundations of manhood for the purpose of application with a 'huddle' of other men for the purpose of implementing proven truths to live out as men. For such a time as this."

Brian Yost—Collaborator, Connector and Co-founder CITYCommit

"Why do so many men fail at life? They haven't read the playbook. They don't recognize the coach's voice. Former NFL quarterback Jeff Kemp has written a readable, practical guide for men who are ready to start winning. This book is for regular guys who want to be better men! I got a lot from this book."

David Murrow—The Online Preaching Coach and author of *Why Men Hate Going to Church*

"For years I wanted the fulfilled life found with God but surrender to Christ terrified me. I had yet to learn what it looked like. Finally, a book describes surrender to Jesus so that men can receive it. Beware! It's counterintuitive. My buddy, Jeff, will challenge you to abandon the 'be more, do more, have more, get more' lifestyle for one to receive and be like Jesus."

Dr. Johnny Parker—Turn the Page Leadership, The Parker Group

"Jeff's passion for men becoming the man that God has created them to be is inspiring. I know no one more concerned about getting men together to sharpen one another into godly husbands and dads. Every time I am around Jeff, I leave fired up to live as the man God has called me to be. This book will not only inspire you, but it will also equip you to live as God intended you to live."

Dave Wilson—*FamilyLife Today* host and author of *No Perfect Parents*

RECEIVE

The Way of Jesus for Men

JEFF KEMP

Foreword by Tony Dungy

Copyright © 2023 Jeff Kemp

RECEIVE—The Way of Jesus for Men

All Scripture quotations, unless otherwise indicated, are taken from the Holy Bible, New International Version®, NIV®. Copyright ©1973, 1978, 1984, 2011 by Biblica, Inc. Used by permission of Zondervan. All rights reserved worldwide. www.zondervan.com The "NIV" and "New International Version" are trademarks registered in the United States Patent and Trademark Office by Biblica, Inc.

Trade Paperback ISBN: 978-1-7354817-3-9
Trade Hardcover ISBN: 978-1-7354817-5-3
e-Book ISBN: 978-1-7354817-4-6

Published globally by Manhood Journey Press, an imprint of Manhood Journey, Inc., 212 Prestwick Place, Louisville, Kentucky 40243. Manhood Journey and the Father & Son Circle Logo are both registered trademarks of Manhood Journey, Inc. All rights reserved.

No portion of this book may be reproduced or transmitted in any form or by any means, electronic or mechanical, including photocopying and recording, or by any information storage and retrieval system, without permission in writing from the publisher.

Printed in the United States of America.

SPECIAL SALES

Copies of *Receive* can be purchased at special quantity discounts when purchased in bulk by corporations, educational institutions, churches, and other groups. Contact the publisher for information at info@manhoodjourney.org.

Dedication

This book is for each of us men who want real answers to
gut questions like:
Do I measure up?
Am I a good man?
Am I living in a way that matters?
Is it all on me or is there a better way?

This message and book belong to our perfect Father God.
I dedicate it to every young guy, and all men, who have yet
to fully receive what the Father offers us in His Son: our identity as
His adopted son, with His acceptance, freedom, and powerful
presence to be the man you are meant to be.

CONTENTS

FOREWORD
Coach Tony Dungy

J eff Kemp and I have been friends for quite some time, in part because we share similar backgrounds. We both grew up around football and spent time in the National Football League. We saw the insecurity—fueled by injuries, failure, and rejection—and fabricated identities of achievement, status, and fame. Gratefully, early on in the NFL, we both encountered Jesus Christ. His love would impact us as we grew as athletes, and as men. The lessons we learned from our coaches and teammates about the game became intertwined with the lessons we learned about life and manhood from many spiritual mentors. Those are the things Jeff shares with you in *Receive*.

This book's message on manhood is critical for us today. The idea of what real manhood is has been twisted and confused so much that many of us don't know what it means to be a man, let alone know how to get there. Jeff not only gives us God's blueprint of what real manhood looks like, but he presents the game plan we need to reach that goal.

One of the first things you learn when you join a football team is that you can't win games by yourself. Becoming a champion takes an entire team. A big part of that process involves the veteran players showing the young players what it takes. The same thing is true in life. If we want to grow, develop, and reach our potential as men, it will take a team effort.

And it's the responsibility of the more mature men to show the young guys how to navigate the tricky areas of life.

This book shows us how to do that. It does not contain a list of things you need to DO to be a better man. It goes much deeper than that. It's about BEING a man. Jeff explains that we have to develop a mindset about who we **are** that will impact what we **do**. That sense of who we are can get manipulated by what we see in our society or culture. It can get rocked by disappointments or setbacks. But those things shouldn't define us. We need to have a rock-solid foundation so that we know who we are no matter what is going on around us.

And where does that foundation come from? It would be great if you had the benefit of having an awesome dad who showed you the ropes and poured his time and effort into you as you were growing up. But not all of us have had that blessing. Jeff wants you to know that even if you didn't grow up with that dad role model, you can still have a secure and strong identity as a man by getting it directly from the Lord. As you read this book, you'll see that God has not only defined real manhood for us, but He's given us the perfect role model to follow in Jesus.

I hope you will not only dig into this book, but that you'll do it with a friend or two. Give it to guys around you. I pray it becomes a brotherhood experience as you take some buddies with you on a great journey. Like football, manhood is a team sport.

Tony Dungy

INTRODUCTION

"What's it really mean to be a man?"

We cannot afford to keep living in the dark shadows of confusion, insecurity and isolation. There's too much carnage piling up from missing fathers. Counterfeit masculinity and accidental manhood are failing us. You've seen it around you; maybe you've seen it in your own life.

We urgently need a crystal-clear answer and there is one. You can live well as a man, but only when you know your identity and the essential vision of manhood.

I hope you quickly figure out this is not a "just do better" message.

I'm going to encourage you and give you a solid hope and a reliable game plan. But, more than anything, you need a true identity. I can't give you that, but I can point you to the original source. He gives us our identity and He is the clear vision for finding benevolent manhood.

> My identity is received, not achieved.

I'm glad you're reading my book, but my goal is not that you hear from me. It's that you hear from your true Father. I hope you hear His message to you and take away one major truth. That truth is—

You don't have to earn your identity or prove your manhood.
Your identity is received, not achieved.

You don't have to do the heavy lifting of manhood or overcome the challenges of life alone. In fact, you can't. It really is about receiving.

I invite you to open your heart and mind. Get ready to break some paradigms. Let go of the pressure you've been under and receive the freedom to escape the drag of your past.

Manhood is a journey of receiving from God, teaming up with friends, transforming for good and lifting others. But you're not taking this journey by yourself. As Coach Tony said, manhood is a team sport. Don't try it alone. Have some fun and huddle up with a couple of friends. Get real. Talk about your lives. Go deep. Give them the book as an investment in other guys.

Together, you'll be shifting culture's idea of manhood. We'll be the start of a revival of real manhood, manhood that's good for all.

RECEIVE

1

BLITZ ON MEN

I've been investing in a friendship with a guy who's been facing the worst blitz of his life. He's a gifted, magnetic leader, a make-it-happen-no-matter-what kind of guy. He had great success coaching on the college level, more than most of his peers.

Then, out of the blue, the job ended. His career hit a brick wall. Near-term options disappeared. The bandwagon emptied. The phone went quiet.

Success was great—until it wasn't. His identity, or what he had allowed to become his identity, disappeared.

Sometimes performance, and the success that it will hopefully bring, seems like the only path available to a man to define himself. When that possibility is shut down, he's left to stumble and tumble, hoping to find something else that he's good at. Some other source of identity and confidence that will prove to be just as unreliable as the one before it.

You and I have been blitzed. Our brothers, friends, and sons have been blitzed. Even our dads have been blitzed.

Contrary to cultural messaging, toxic masculinity is not to blame. Obviously, too many damaged men are toxic, but they're the outliers. True masculinity—responsibility and strength inclined to help and protect others—is good. What's toxic is a culture that torpedoes true masculinity and cancels real manhood.

> Our toxic culture stands in the way of true masculinity—the responsible strength to help and protect others.

Society has lost the vision of manhood and it's up to us to restore it. Not by force but by living it out. And to do that, we need to make sure that we're sourcing our identity from the right place.

COUNTERING THE BLITZ

Here are the essentials of a real and good masculine identity:

1. It comes from being made in God's image.
2. It is developed by following the example of Jesus.
3. It is received, not achieved.
4. It focuses on benefiting others.
5. It operates best within a team.

Behind the blitz on masculinity there's a crisis of identity. The perception that many guys, and maybe most, have of themselves, and their quest to find a better one, came from childhood. Mostly from the relationship with their dad. But the big point that I want to make is this:

Our true identity is received from our Father in heaven.

Whether we had an affirming dad, a neglectful, absent or even abusive dad, every one of us has access to a perfect Dad. He designed you. He proved His love for you and invited you to be His adopted son when you receive His beloved Son Jesus whom He offered as the ultimate and complete solution.

Without receiving our identity and manhood as an unconditionally loved and accepted son of our perfect Father in Heaven, we will wander and work to prove ourselves in a myriad of ways that will never satisfy and are guaranteed to bring an unhappy ending.

The Father's epic invitation changes lives and destinies when we accept it.

The good news about blitzes is they're not just painful and negative. Having faced many blitzes in football, I know they can cause sacks, fumbles, interceptions, and concussions. But they can also result in game-changing touchdowns. Blitzes can trigger transformation. Blitzes are like a crisis—danger and opportunity in the same package. It all depends on perspective and the willingness to change. This book is a book about reality and hope. If you find yourself faking it, dogged by doubts and latent flaws, or if you feel discouraged and disqualified to be the man you want to be, you're not alone. We've been trying to figure out manhood for generations. Our culture has been selling us counterfeits of manhood with catastrophic flaws.

> Achievement-earned identity and fame are the embedded Kryptonite for most men.

That's what my buddy is going through in a brutally intense way. He had an oversized father wound. By going all-in to succeed at an elite level, he built a super-sized performance ego and achievement identity. He chased one of the counterfeit scripts for manhood being all about success and winning. And he won big—for a while. Achievement-earned identity and fame rarely delivers on the promise. The embedded Kryptonite for most men is pride.

But we have a role model who is fully real and fully good. He doesn't leave us on our own. He will give us His ability to be authentic and beneficial to others. No matter the type of father we have—or even if we experienced an absent-father childhood—we all have a perfect Father. We can be accepted and affirmed by Him. It doesn't depend on our ability to figure it all out or perform.

That's what's happened for my buddy. It took a mega blitz for him to hit his bottom, but a God-sized comprehensive turnaround story is underway. God has reached Him.

The blitz brought reality and, eventually, humility. Humility brought him to God on God's terms. Father God gave him his real identity, his true identity. It's not performance or achievement based. It's not conditional. It's not earned. It's secure. It can't be lost.

He's realized that he didn't invent or create himself. God did. He now knows that God is present and personal. He's a Father and a very good one at that. He's now receiving and experiencing the love of his perfect Father. Though his ego and depression lengthened his brutal journey through the dark valley of the shadows, Father God patiently kept welcoming him home. Despite intense shock, ego-fueled anger, and depression that pinned him to the floor, he stayed faithful to his family and desperately turned to a couple of loyal friends for help. He ran out of his own solutions. His legendary self-will failed him. He quit running his life. He let God take over. He's thriving without the addictively dominating career and externally defined identity.

He's experienced the hope that is true for every single one of us, no matter our story. When he faced his emptiness, humbled himself to receive Jesus as his sole answer, he became the perfect Father's son. That's who he is.

That's what we'll explore throughout this book.

ASK MYSELF

- "Who and what has shaped my view of manhood and success?"

MY ACTION

- I will call a trusted friend or approachable, mature man and say something like this, "I'd like to talk with you occasionally about the journey of manhood as I read this book." Go from there.

"What is belittling, wounding and damaging young men today? Always trying to prove themselves through a lot of avenues that will never really prove themselves, never satisfy, never get there. A never-ending chase to get approval of somebody else. Whenever they fall short, they don't have another man, a father or father figure to say, 'I'm proud of you and you have what it takes.'"

> I can't become what I can't define.

—**Benjamin Watson, retired NFL tight end**

"If you could open a man and see his vision, you'll see his whole life. You can't become what you can't define. Men are drowning in a black hole, a culture without older men giving the vision and fathers calling them into manhood."

—**Robert Lewis**

2

IDENTITY THEFT

I remember being afraid of losing races or wrestling matches or of getting "out" in a game of dodgeball. I wasn't afraid of playing, or even of getting hurt. But I was afraid of losing.

And girls? Whoa! Talk about fear. There was this cute blond classmate who lived in our neighborhood. Every morning as we walked to school I wanted to catch up and walk beside her. But I could never get up the courage, so I followed at a safe distance of 20 yards. Every morning. I know—stupid!

Insecurity dogged me in college, too. I wouldn't show my face at a frat party until I'd gotten a buzz at my own frat first. I could *act* cocky, but I was actually super insecure and self-conscious. I cared way too much about what people thought of me.

I hated that feeling and I hated being the kind of person that it made me—a follower, a compromiser, a withholder. I missed many opportunities to really get to know people. I was too worried about what they might have been thinking about me. I was more concerned with *being* interesting than I was about *showing* interest in others.

As I've since moved through various seasons of life, I see what the insecurity did to me. It caused me to adopt a performance-oriented identity to try to compensate. But my cure only made the disease worse.

So, who else has been insecure? You? Probably. Maybe the current of insecurity still runs strong in you.

IDENTITY VERSUS IMAGE

What many call *identity* is really *image*. Identity is who we are deep down inside, but image is the way we "sell ourselves" to others. It's how we want to be perceived, our brand. It's the cheap knockoff we settle for when we think the real thing doesn't measure up.

> "Image" is what I sell to others. "Identity" is who I am deep down inside.

Image has become a big deal, affecting how we feel about ourselves and shaping the expectations we have in life. Just a few generations ago, image was a non-issue. Identity was the whole equation of who a person was. But with industrialization and the rapid expanse of travel and communication, we were exposed to far more people than family and neighbors. And comparison went into hyper-drive.

Comparison has always been a driver of human insecurity. The inward push to make a good impression, to fit in, or even to come off as the leader of the pack are all connected to the way we socialize. It's no surprise, then, that image is now of greater importance than identity. Identity (who we are) has given the wheel to image (who we want others to think we are—our "brand").

That's a bad thing.

Growing up, image had a big impact on me. My dad was a successful and highly visible man. His mantra to me was, "You're a Kemp—Be a leader." I believed I had to be like him. I felt that it was my legacy to be influential like he was. To get there I would need to start succeeding—proving myself, becoming popular, and impressing people. In my mind my performance was constantly being evaluated and I was judged according to wins and losses—in every setting, not just football. After all, Dad had been a 13-year pro quarterback and league MVP. He had won two championships quarterbacking the Buffalo Bills. Then he became a congressman and went on to have great influence in the political arena. I needed a bunch of my own successes to match his. I felt it, I wanted it, and, to my way of thinking, everyone expected it.

In reality, my parents were great. They didn't pressure me, but I did enough of that for myself and them.

It started young. I remember feeling like a zero on the eighth-grade football team when I tried to become the quarterback but never rose above second-string. I really wanted to feel accepted and impressive to the team, but I couldn't see doing that as the backup. Even though I loved football, I quit that year. I gave my parents what I thought was an admirable excuse: I wanted to concentrate on my grades. Looking back, Dad could have chuckled or pressed me, but he didn't.

My insecure feelings continued when I tried again in my junior year at a new high school, but this time ended up as the third-string quarterback. (I was losing ground!) And I repeated the mediocrity as a sophomore at Dartmouth College. Throughout grade school, junior high, high school, and into college, my performance didn't meet my expectations. And if it didn't meet mine, I was sure it didn't meet anyone else's. (Insecurity tells us all kinds of lies like that.)

I felt like my identity had been stolen. Jeff Kemp was supposed to be a winner.

MY IDENTITY SCRIPT

Being an insecure overachiever, I had to make a plan. I needed a script that would line out for me exactly what I could do to achieve the success I craved. If winning in life was my destiny, hard work and perseverance would be my path. And I was okay with that.

In my mind, following the script would ensure that I would excel as a student, as an athlete, as a friend, as a leader, and as a Christian. I would get good grades, make starting quarterback, get drafted into the NFL, be popular, and make a difference.

Do you have an identity script? I don't mean one that's written down somewhere, and I don't mean a set of goals you have for making yourself a truly better man. I'm referring to the stuff you think you must do in order to have value, the things that if you don't do, you'll be a big fat zero: Win awards. Own a bunch of stuff. Marry the babe. Have cute babies that grow up to be the popular kids. Be the life of the party. Have the lowest handicap. Be connected.

> Who writes my "identity script"?

You'll wear yourself out following a script like that. You'll never rest in your identity if you're constantly trying to build an image.

A WIG AND A CHAMELEON

Andre Agassi's childhood was an all-out strategy to create an elite professional athlete. He was driven to the max—with his dad in the driver's seat. Eventually, Andre did master the tennis court. He also mastered endorsement advertising, leveraging his fame to market Canon cameras. Their iconic, and ironic, phrase was, "Image is everything."

But image was no more reality for Andre than it is for you or me.

Andre's image was accented by his long flowing blond hair. But he went bald at a young age and began wearing a wig to keep the image alive. He eventually faced a moment of panic during a match because he feared that his wig—which he had damaged in the shower earlier in the day— would fly off his head while playing. That day, fear of losing his image distracted him and he lost the match.

That story seemed crazy to me until I realized the size of the image Andre was trying to live up to. Then I thought about my own insecurities and how I'd tried to project an impressive image. Andre wore a wig; I became a chameleon. I adapted my image to please the people I was with. When I was around my parents, people from the church, or coaches, I was a "good guy." When I was with the fraternity crowd, I was a carefree partier.

A big part of my image-protecting strategy involved pretending to be nonchalant about my passion to play pro football. I played it cool. I didn't let on to my dad or others that it was incredibly important to me. I didn't want them focusing on the miniscule chance of my getting a shot in the NFL, and I certainly wanted to avoid the embarrassment of failing in my dream if it didn't happen. If I did make it into the league, I was prepared to appear cool and confident, like I knew all along that it would turn out this way. And then, after I actually made it into the NFL, I acted so comfortable with it that I hesitated to ask some of the veteran players to mentor me and give me some pointers. I could have reached out for help, but image held me back.

> There is a high cost of confusing image and identity.

For Andre Agassi, for me, and maybe for you, confusing image for identity proved costly. Even the successes were tainted, leaving us empty, dissatisfied, anxious, and even more self-conscious.

Image is unreliable. Nobody is perfect and therefore every image we concoct is compromised from the start. We simply cannot live up to our own expectations or deliver on the hopes we've created. We will lose games. We will miss the cut. Someone else will get the promotion. Every perfect season will be followed by an imperfect one. We will put numbers in both the wins and losses columns.

Confusing image for identity is at the root of many guys' struggles and many men's downfalls. It's common for us to trip over our hypocrisy (that's a big part of what image is), yet it doesn't have to be fatal. Realizing what image-making and image-protecting can do is one of the keys to waking up sooner so we can escape the trap. And once we do that, we can move in a healthier direction.

The more we think about ourselves in terms of image and the more energy and emotion we put into cultivating that image, the more likely we are to delay or miss becoming our true selves and who God made us to be.

IMAGE AND GOD?

Yes, I just brought God into the conversation.

If you have the perspective that God isn't relevant or real, I'm glad you're reading this book. I hope you'll keep an open mind. I've seen in my own life, and in others, that shaping life around what others think of us creates an unhealthy pride, nagging insecurity, and weak character. I believe we need reliable help to understand who we are—and that would take us back to the source, to where we came from, to who made us, and to why we were made.

> We were never meant to be image-makers, but image-bearers.

Shaping our lives through image doesn't work well. Here's why: We were never meant to be image-*makers*. We are image-*bearers*.

The God who made us is a God of relationships and communication. In the beginning of His written communication, the Bible, He says, "So God created man in his own image . . ." (Genesis 1:27 ESV). This means that who I am is found in discovering who God is.

Receiving our identity from this God who created us—and loves us—is the truth that transcends everything else about us. It has far greater implications than our background, position,

> imagine the freedom of living *from* my identity (received from God) rather than *for* it.

popularity, or performance. More than our looks, talents, ethnicity, or marital status. It can securely anchor the way we see ourselves and how we relate to others. Being an image-bearer of God is the core of our identity, the essence of who we are and who we can become. We will talk more about that in chapter 8.

Imagine the freedom of living *from* your identity rather than *for* it. Imagine the great feeling of not having to pretend to be someone you're not. Imagine the better man you can be just by being real.

ASK MYSELF

- "What's my identity script—the stuff I think I need to do, achieve, have, or project to feel okay about myself?"
- "Do I view who I am by performance and image or by unchanging relationships?"

MY ACTIONS

- I need to figure out my story.
- I will write down key events that have shaped how I view myself.

> Image imitates identity but prevents security. Identity is received, not achieved.

- I will examine my story with its identity deficits and pay attention to the ways I've been driven to try to "earn" my identity. I will write down the key events, dominant emotions, and interactions that have marked my life. I will even set out to diagram these shaping events and chapters chrono-logically. (For a sample, visit www.menhuddle.com.)
- I'll talk with a mentor about this or get his help in doing it.

Image imitates identity but prevents security. Identity is received, not achieved.

3

A MAN'S JOURNEY

’m living proof that a guy can grow up in a supportive home and still be dogged by insecurity. Two childhood memories stand out.

The first happened in fifth grade. Our PE department held a wrestling match, and I was eager to prove myself as an athlete. My dad had invited his friend Eddie Rutkowski, a former All-American wrestler for Notre Dame University. Impressing him was all that mattered to me that day. But I lost. And then I cried because I was shattered in front of Dad and Eddie.

Then, in tenth grade, there was the girl I mentioned earlier. (Few things can make us as insecure as wondering if a girl likes us, right?)

Every morning, we walked to our high school . . . but not together. Most days, I'd walk behind her, dying to stride up to walk and talk with her, but I never found the courage. All year, I lagged behind, held back by my insecurity.

INSECURITY RETURNS

Insecurity isn't just a childhood illness. Many years after my cowardly slow-paced walk to school, my insecurity came calling again. I was ten years into my quarterbacking career when some friends, Dave and Kathy, invited Stacy and me to go bowling. I may have been a professional athlete, but bowling was not in my wheelhouse. It was in Dave's. He was good, I'd never seen anyone roll the ball that fast and accurately.

My competitiveness and my insecurity collided that night, and it wasn't pretty. I bowled my lowest game since childhood. I tried to rocket the ball as hard as Dave and threw more gutter balls than anything else. Stacy saw my little-boy insecurity working against me. My drive to match Jerry's power made me lose—and look like a junior high idiot.

Does any of this feel familiar? Are insecurity and self-consciousness wrapped around your axle too?

Relax. We've all been there. Most of us wonder what other people think of us. We worry about impressing both friends and strangers. We desperately want to fit in. We'll change our behavior if we think it will help us make the desired impression. And that's when the real trouble begins.

As the "audience" changes, we adapt our behavior to fit or impress. When we're with work colleagues, we're this guy. When we're with church friends, we're another guy. Dudes from the neighborhood make us yet another guy. And reunions with old college buddies? Hey, that's inviting some serious exaggeration. It's audience-driven schizophrenia.

> Adapting my behavior to fit in or impress can confuse my sense of identity.

We're so many different personas that we aren't sure who we really are. We interpret what we think others want from us and then morph into it for the current situation. Problem is, this ultimately results in a flawed and highly unstable view of ourselves.

WHERE WE'VE COME FROM

Like every journey, this journey of manhood has a beginning that determines your path. Understanding where you started will help you know where you need to go.

I'm not throwing stones at anyone's family and home, but more often than not, the family that raised us is where our problems start. So, as we try to move forward in our journey, it's helpful to look back over the ground we've covered to see what could have been done differently—by us and by those who shaped us.

Of course, we wish our parents had made our early years easier—if dad had been there, if mom and dad's relationship were healthy or if they'd engaged more in developing us from a boy into an emerging man. But no one has a perfect family and our parents' childhood wasn't perfect either. Theirs was just as painful and deficient as ours, maybe more.

> Retracing my family history might reveal the works of God in my life.

So, without dwelling on the past or holding on to resentment, look back with mercy on your family and upbringing. How has it impacted your identity and sowed insecure, self-conscious thoughts?

Retrace your steps. You might see how God has been involved throughout your life, sometimes without you knowing. I've sat with many guys as they've unpacked their stories and found themselves amazed, and even choked up, when they realized that God had already been fathering them, through some dark, difficult early chapters in their story.

But there's good news. You don't have to live out the remainder of your life lagging behind!

It might sound counter-intuitive, but your journey of manhood is becoming a son again (as you'll learn more about in Chapter 6).

SEASONS

Every man's journey from *AS IS* to *TO BE* happens gradually over the course of his life—through many seasons.

Robert Lewis is a friend and mentor of mine. His teaching and coaching have helped hundreds of men. Drawing from what Robert shared with me about our inner man, let's identify four seasons of a man's journey.

> The season of STRUGGLE selfishly involves positioning myself to win and feel good.

The first season is *Struggle.* This is when we try things on our own, wrestle with insecurities, and try to position ourselves to win and feel good. But it's like winter. We slip, slide, and crash. We can't see the sun.

Even though it's a hard season, we shouldn't dismiss the importance of struggle. It's the primary way that we learn and become humble and vulnerable enough to talk about our lives—an important bridge to bonding with others and positively impacting them. Because we *all* struggle.

> The season of SURRENDER teaches me grace and true sonship.

Next is the season of *Surrender.* We begin to understand that we didn't invent ourselves and we don't need to run our own life. Frankly, we can't. We learn how to become the son of a Perfect Father. We discover grace; God has invited us to come to Him and receive His unconditional love and constant guidance. That's real sonship!

Then comes the season of *Significance.* We find *our* purpose and mission in relation to *God's* purpose and mission. We figure out how our gifts, talents, passions, and story are repurposed to be beneficial in the lives of others. We start living to make our part of the world better. Our surrender and connection to God is met with Him changing us and producing good character and good fruit in our lives. It's summer. God heals, brings growth, and produces good things in us and through us. We become men who live for others.

> The season of SIGNIFICANCE is living my purpose within God's mission for my life.

Finally, the season of *Satisfaction and Sharing*. We are matured, grateful, and others-centered. We've learned and progressed. We've seen our worst chapters rewritten and it's time to share what we've learned in our story and to build up new leaders and a new generation. This is mentoring and giving back. This is fall, when a full harvest is gratefully shared with family, those with needs, and up-and-coming leaders.

> The season of SATISFACTION and SHARING: My story has been rewritten, and I enjoy investing in others.

MY STRUGGLE AND SURRENDER

Let me tell you a little about my own season of *Struggle* that led me to *Surrender*. Ironically, it was two years of success, popularity, and unbridled fun that prompted me to discover my need to surrender.

My last two years of college went way better than my first two. Junior and senior years were a blast. Going into my junior year, I wanted to be popular and confident, and have girls like me. Mainly, I wanted to be a great quarterback. I had this notion that being a great quarterback would fix all my other deficiencies and desires. I was an insecure, self-conscious, competitive, hard-working "good guy" who wanted only to succeed and feel good about myself. I took more than a few character shortcuts to try to prop up my confidence. Junior year, some of what I wanted started happening. Things went well. I wasn't yet great, but I was having some success and a lot of fun.

Just before graduation, I felt that I had everything I wanted: football, an impressive college degree, fraternity friends, girlfriends, popularity, and a shot at the NFL and becoming a Los Angeles Ram. My life was the best it had ever been.

But during a week of partying before graduation, I had a life-changing shift of seasons—even though I was drunk most of the time. I was having more fun than ever, but I wasn't happy with who I was. I was disguising my insecurities. My character was at an all-time low. There was a selfish thread running through how I treated people, girlfriends, and my buddies.

I was privately afraid of getting cut by the Rams and losing out on my dream.

> Is God tracking me down and looking to change me?

What I now realize is that God was tracking me down and inviting me to Himself. At the time my only purpose was me—loving myself and my dreams more than anything else. Despite the success I gained, I had this emptiness in me. Suddenly, surrendering to God, trusting Him, and aiming for His purposes for my life made sense. I didn't know much, but I knew that I wanted to let God change me.

He was giving me a gift, inviting me to leave the cold winter of *Struggle* to enter the refreshing spring of *Surrender*. That week, as I left college and headed off to California, I made the decision to surrender control and take up Jesus as my purpose.

THE DIFFERENCE MAKER: A GUIDE

The journey of manhood is a quest to receive your identity and live *from* it rather than *for* it. It's a journey to find your purpose, to become secure in who you are and able to live in a responsible way that makes a positive impact and difference. It's figuring out how to be faithful and true, loyal and honest, trustworthy and authentic.

If you're like me, you hear a charge like that and you're ready to go for it–until you try and find out you're not ready. Not because you don't want to be these things or that you aren't sincere in your desire for them. It's just that—you can't live up to it. You need help. This journey is not to be taken alone.

I don't do well with "some assembly required" projects. I might struggle through putting together a gas grill, even if I follow the multipage, fine-print instructions. There may be a few parts left over. And the grill might wobble a bit. I'm not the guy to fix your faucet, lawn mower, or glitchy computer setup.

But there are a couple things in life that I excelled at—like snow skiing and throwing a football. For those, I didn't have a list of instructions, but I didn't wing it either. I had a model. A really good model. I lived in his house. I was his son.

I started skiing with Dad at a small icy ski area in Buffalo, New York, all winter long, from the time I was four until Dad's cancer in 2008. Dad eventually took our family on annual trips to Vail and before that, Snowmass, Colorado, where he encouraged me to copy his friend and Olympic champion Stein Erickson by skiing behind him. I copied what I saw modeled.

When it came to passing the football, Dad didn't tell me how to throw—he showed me. He molded my fingers to the laces. He reached around me to position the ball near my chest. He modeled a quick release and strong spiral. I picked it up, improved and loved it. I had a model.

> Jesus—the model of a man.

Even better, I had a loving relationship with the model.

Great news! You've got an awesome model of manhood. You're even related to Him. But He doesn't force the relationship upon you. (And sadly, many of us miss it for much of our life.)

Jesus is your model. He was the quintessential man, the strongest, most courageous, most influential, and most successful man in history. And the most humble, sacrificial, and relational man ever.

- He respected his parents, but always gravitated toward His Father in Heaven.
- He stepped out of boyhood into being responsible for himself. He stuck close to the Father, awaiting the timing and steps of his mission.
- He built friendships, invested in relationships, developed a team, and trained leaders who served.
- He faced life head-on, especially rejection, suffering, and even death. He paid the price for eventual triumph and transcending victory.
- He was real—honest, authentic, approachable, vulnerable. He noticed and showed emotion. He was truthful. He lived true.
- He had pure motives and was dependably loyal. He lived faithfully.
- He was all love and all truth, all the time.

SEE IT IN ACTION—RUSSELL WILSON'S STORY

I had a conversation with a fellow former Seahawk QB Russell Wilson before he was traded to the Broncos. His journey of manhood has the hallmarks we've been talking about.

"One of the scriptures I really love is First Corinthians 13. It talks about going from a child to a man—getting rid of childish things. I think that as I went through a lot early in life that God was preparing me."

Looking back at our youth and God's work in it can be the first step in a man's journey. For Russell, that was remembering that he was a troublemaker—a kid who pretty much only loved sports. But God had a plan for transforming him into the man and leader that he is today.

Russell had a troubling dream of his dad passing away; God had caught his attention. "I remember that dream vividly. My family always went to church and the next day was Sunday. That's when I was saved."

Like my own story, God had invited Russell into the relationship that would become the foundation for his life. His life changed and growing up accelerated.

Then, Russell met his first guide: one of his teachers. Booker Corrigan took an interest in this little athlete and not-so-great student who was getting into too much trouble. With high school and college just around the corner, Booker spoke to Russell with honesty and vision. He told Russell, "If you put as much attention, love and passion into your schoolwork and people as you do into sports, how far will you go?"

Russell remembers it as another turning point. "That perspective changed my life. From there, literally, immediately my life changed, as it talks about in the Bible how God can change anything immediately. I vividly remember that. That's when I kind of changed my life in high school."

He focused on both school and sports. Both went well. In college, he learned to focus on others and treat them well by serving. And ever since his rookie season in the NFL, Russell visited the seriously ill children at the Seattle Children's Hospital every week during the unreal pace and pressures of the NFL season!

"When I got into the NFL, visiting the kids taught me a lot about what love looked like—the caring and serving that Jesus did," Russell reflects. "That was big for me. If I try to describe my life in one word, it'd be the word 'love.' And I say that because, you know, going back to First Corinthians 13, it says 'if I have all these things, but I don't have this one thing—love—I have nothing.'"

Russell's journey of manhood took him from the little troublemaker who only focused on his own sports ambitions to a man who strives first to care and serve like Jesus.

You might be thinking, "But how do I get my vision for manhood?"

In the next chapter, we'll look at Jesus' ultimate model for manhood.

> I can have it all—but
> if I don't have love,
> I have nothing.

ASK MYSELF

- "What season am I in: STRUGGLE, SURRENDER, SIGNIFICANCE or SATISFACTION & SHARING?"
- "Who will I seek for help to rewrite my identity script and clarify my vision for manhood?"

MY ACTIONS

- I will ask God: What do I need to understand about my dad's and mom's backstories and how my own childhood was affected by them?
- I will talk with a friend or mentor about my childhood and how it may have shaped my insecurities and identity quest.

"Vision and relationships are the twin towers of manhood."
—Robert Lewis

"My goal, my dreams, my life—God, it's gotta be more than this."
—Tom Brady when asked how great it was to win three Super Bowls by 27. (Sixty Minutes interview, 2005)

4

THE ULTIMATE MAN

Is there a timeless and universal essence of manhood? An ideal example? A model that works for each guy in every culture for all time?

I say, yes. A quintessential man *has* walked the earth. His name is Jesus.

When looking for a blueprint of masculinity, it only makes sense to look to the source–the way God Himself took on the form of man when He lived here for 33 years.

I don't know what you think of Him, but you should know that I like Jesus—a lot! I'm a follower of Jesus. I'm a Christian. I base my life and my future on Him being my Savior and the Christ—God's chosen Messiah sent to save all. My faith is not in religion or any flavor of church, though I greatly value and participate in the church Stacy and I attend. My faith is not in trying to be good enough for God. I look to Jesus as the center point of history, and my personal solution and Lord. I believe He is both a revolutionary and the ultimate source of peace.

THE ULTIMATE MAN

But right now, I'm writing about the vision for manhood. I'm pointing to Him as a man who was real and good, the greatest man. The ultimate man and role model. Focusing on Jesus can give us the complete picture and essential game plan for authentic manhood. He is the one who knows the most about being a man, so we can make progress in our own journey as men by considering Him.

> Jesus Christ: the ultimate man and role model.

In the Spring of 2020, I decided to read slowly and intentionally the story of Jesus' life in the first four books of the New Testament. Over a couple of months, I observed 221 ways Jesus lived that apply to manhood. But before I share some of these, I need to say that looking at the type of man Jesus was can be done in the wrong way.

Comparing your traits to His and then flunking yourself out is the wrong way. Seeing how great and perfect He was and thinking, "I stink. I suck. I've blown it. I can't be like that. I need to fake it" is the wrong way. Comparing yourself to Him and feeling buried and trapped in shame is the wrong way.

And while we're on that topic, let's pull up for a minute and talk about shame. Improperly handled, shame becomes a hopeless identity. It's one of the devil's big weapons. It's the language he uses when he tries to convince you that you are bad and always will be bad. Even worthless. Unforgivable. Beyond changing.

CONVICTION VERSUS SHAME

God uses a different language: conviction. While shame says, "You are bad. You're guilty and hopeless," conviction says, "You did bad. You fall short, but with Me you can get back on track." The language of shame and the language of conviction say completely different things. The devil,

through shame, condemns and disqual-
ifies. God, through conviction, offers
forgiveness and help.

> Shame condemns and
> disqualifies change.
> Conviction offers hope
> and forgiveness.

So, before you read this and compare your messed-up manhood with the
perfect man that Jesus was, remember:
Jesus was God in a body. His standard

is beyond your reach, and mine, but His forgiveness, friendship and empowering help are not.

We're not striving for "Junior Jesus Perfection" status in hopes that we can impress God into giving us a break or a bonus. As men, we are already loved by our Father God who has offered us both a Savior and a brother in Jesus.

FEEDING THE 5,000

Through so many of the things He did and said while on earth, we know that Jesus was a man of mission and relationships. He embodied adventure, friendship, and teamwork. Yes, first and foremost He was—and is—the Son of the Heavenly Father. But the interaction of His God-ness *and* His man-ness can be seen in every day of the 33 years He lived among us.

Let's drop in on one of those days—an intense day famously recounted in all four gospels.

Two big things happened. First, Jesus' disciples had just gotten off the road and were reporting on their mission and experiences. They got so carried away talking about what happened that they forgot to eat. Jesus, always an attentive and caring leader, tuned into their stories and their needs. He saw that these guys needed to pull away from crowds to rest and refuel.

Jesus needed to refuel too. Whenever people heard that he was in their region, they flocked to hear him and ask for help. So, he'd been teaching, healing, and meeting all kinds of needs and crises. And, let's face it, people can be exhausting.

The other thing that had happened was that Jesus had received news that his friend and cousin, John the Baptist, had been ruthlessly beheaded. John was a man Jesus had depended on, the one man with the guts to proclaim Jesus as the Son of God (which was not well received by most people, especially the proud religious ones).

So, here's Jesus with his disciples—tired, grieving, and needing a break.

The Bible says that Jesus and his men then "slipped away" by boat on their way to a "desolate place." But the people figured out where they were going and walked there to meet them. Imagine how you'd feel if you were trying to retreat with your friends and 5,000+ people show up—not only demanding your attention but truly needing it.

Jesus graciously adapted. He felt compassion for the people, and he welcomed them. Let me repeat: He *welcomed* them. He then began to heal those who needed it, and he taught the crowd the hopeful truth about God's kingdom.

It was more than a full day; it was a non-stop day. And now, late in the evening, they were all hungry. *All* of them. That's 5,000+ people, in a desolate place—no inns, taverns, restaurants, or food trucks. The disciples urged Jesus to send the people away to find food and a place to sleep.

But Jesus didn't see limitations and He wasn't in the habit of sending people away.

JESUS' BETTER PLAN

He always listened to His Father. They had a better plan. Jesus used the crisis as an opportunity. He took His mission to the next level and intensified His training of His team. He told them, basically, *they don't need to go away, you feed them*. Philip, one of the disciples, said what all the others were thinking: *It's impossible.* Then he added, just to make sure Jesus understood how impossible it was: "It would take more than half a year's wages to buy enough bread for each one to have a bite!" (John 6:7).

Another disciple, Andrew, had been doing some recon, but hadn't found much reason to hope. "There's a young boy here with five barley loaves and two fish," he said. "But what good is that with this huge crowd?" (John 6:9 NLT).

Jesus didn't mind shortages, long odds, or situations that seemed out of control. He was about to show his men how to depend on the Father. In fact, they would soon witness a mega-miracle.

Jesus coached his disciples to have the people sit on the ground in groups of fifty. He took the loaves and fish, looked up to His Father in heaven and prayed a blessing over the fish and the bread. And then he gave the food to his disciples and had them carry it out into the crowd to serve the people.

This went on until everyone was fully fed. And get this, the disciples went out into the crowd again and gathered up twelve baskets of leftovers. One basket of leftovers per disciple! More than 5,000 people had shared a single sack lunch . . . and there were leftovers!

WHAT KIND OF MAN IS THIS?

When the sun set on this amazing day, Jesus sent his disciples to the boat so they could go back across the lake while he dismissed the crowds. He then went up alone into the mountains to dialogue and recharge with His Father in Heaven. Connecting to His Father was His priority.

Obviously, Jesus had both a human and a divine nature, but what kind of *man* spent the day serving and then feeding over 5,000? And to cut it closer to the bone, what do we see in Him that people around us would love to see in you and me?

Here are just a few qualities of a real and good man we see in Jesus as He interacted with His disciples and the crowd:

He was a man who was first and foremost a son. He received guidance and strength from His Father. He always identified himself as his Father's son. He willingly depended on His Father. He often said that he was here to do His Father's work and could do nothing apart from His Father.

He was a man with friends. He was trusted by His friends, largely because He invested in His friends and helped them grow. He gave them attention, help, and encouragement—love, in man language. He developed them into friends. Many men take and take and take—but give very little. Jesus gave, and gave, and gave. He invested in them.

He was marked by empathy. He was compassionate toward others. He noticed and met people's physical, emotional, and spiritual needs. He had great concern for people that were sick, hopeless, and oppressed. He went close to those that others avoided.

He was strong for others—a man on a mission to benefit others, to make lives better and ultimately to give life that lasts forever. He persevered and sacrificed to rescue and help others to advance His Father's eternal kingdom mission.

He built a team and trained His men. He didn't work alone. He developed, equipped and stretched His friends. He lifted and launched His team, sending them out to serve, feed and enlighten others. He also prioritized time with them, realizing their need to celebrate, rest and refuel, not just to grind and produce.

He was not upset by redirected plans or intense challenges. He was resilient and adaptable. People were not a burden to him. He didn't make them feel like a bother or an intrusion. Actually, people were often surprised at his eagerness to talk with them, and dignify or help them, even when there was a whirl of activity going on around them.

He was humble, grateful, optimistic, and resourceful. He saw an alternative to sending people away. He thanked the Father in the challenging moment and saw no limits to what His Father could do with a sack lunch.

He was decisive and bold. He trained His disciples with action and intense experiences, not just words and instruction. After their role in the miraculous feeding, He sent them out for a rougher than rough midnight boat ride, capped off by a walk on the water. He guided and equipped his team to grow in faith and transform as men so they could improve the lives of others.

He built community. He formed smaller and more personal groups out of the mob. He sat people down on green grass in groups of fifty rather than keeping them scattered and disconnected from one another. He brought order to chaos, peace to anxiousness.

And that was just one day! Imagine spending a lifetime with Jesus.

But that's for another chapter.

ASK MYSELF

- "Do I have a clear vision of the essence of manhood—of a real and good man? Or am I confused and frustrated, chasing after moving targets?"

MY ACTIONS

- For the next 3-5 days, I will read all four of the biblical accounts of a single day in Jesus' life (Matthew 14:13-33; Mark 6:30-52; Luke 9:10-17; John 6:1-21). As I read, I will ask God for His vision of manhood.

> Jesus is the vision and example for manhood. He modeled compassion, strength, and courage.

"Deep in a man's heart are some fundamental questions that cannot be answered at the kitchen table. Who am I? What am I? What am I destined for? Do I have what it takes?"
—**John Eldredge**

Jesus is the vision for manhood—sonship fueling compassion, strength and courage in a greater cause. He modeled the essence of masculinity—humble, loyal and sacrificial—to provide, protect and reconcile others.

5

IDENTITY FOUND— THE GIDEON PRINCIPLE

In 1987, the San Francisco 49ers traded me to the Seattle Seahawks where I would be the backup to Dave Krieg. Early in my second season there, Dave was injured, and I was called on to start the next game— against the 49ers. It was the opportunity I had waited for. A key offensive coach even pulled me aside before the game and gushed, "I've been waiting for this day that you'd be the Hawks QB, Jeff." I felt an invincible thrill that I could lead my new team to victory and the playoffs. I could become the Seahawks' starter, and even show my former team they'd made a mistake in trading me. (Actually, replacing me with future Hall of Famer Steve Young didn't prove to be much of a mistake for them. HA!)

The game didn't quite go as I'd envisioned. Joe Montana ended up throwing three TD passes, and Steve Young even threw one late in the game. In the first half I only completed four passes (three to the wrong team!). So, being down 17-0 at the half, and having my worst performance ever, my hopes of a career boost were down the drain. I spent the second half of the game and the rest of the season on the sidelines. My coach who had intensely esteemed me before the game didn't even make eye contact or talk with me for weeks to follow. In his eyes, my previously esteemed worth which he'd gushed about had been erased.

FAILURE AND WORTH

I had failed him. I had failed the team. My performance failed in the eyes of a performance-driven conditional society. My vision of success disappeared with my failure and demotion from 1st team to 3rd team QB. If I wasn't a winning quarterback, who was I?

I'm grateful that early in my NFL career I made friends with good men and married an awesome woman. They helped me understand that the answers to those questions of performance and status are found in asking a better question—

Who made me?

I'm not an accident. You're not an accident. No human is. Even if you were a "surprise" to your parents, someone wanted you to exist—and for good reason.

> Because I am made by God, I am valued and loved regardless of my performance.

We have a good designer and a loving creator—God. The eternal God created us in His image. We are souls. Our bodies live only for a while in this life, but our souls live on eternally.

God didn't think less of me when I was benched than He did when I led teams to victory. The coach might have soured on me, but God never did. He made me. He loves me. He gave his only Son to bring me back to Him as His adopted and fully loved son.

God does not think less of you because your dad belittled you, or because you messed up in school, in your career, or in your marriage. He's not defining you by your flaws or addictions. He's not defining you by your losses or by your wins. He sees you as His son who, even though you have strayed, has been invited back into that Father-son relationship He desires to have with you.

> **How I view God and myself gives me my real identity and true worth.**

Counselors know that the view we have of ourselves shapes how we live. I would add: how we view God shapes how we live even more. When we honestly consider where we came from and embrace the truth that God is our perfect Father who created us and redeems us, then we can grasp our real identity and true worth. That changes everything.

After retiring from the NFL, I coached many seasons of youth football. One year we had this shorter, heavyset boy on the team (I'll call him Matt). He was a wonderful kid—nice, sincere, respectful.

We coaches had a code: Don't measure the kids by performance; measure them by their effort and attitude. And Matt had heart. He gave full effort, even if it was harder for him than some kids.

So, practice ends one day. A car pulls up, a guy gets out, and instead of walking over to the field like the other dads, he yells in Matt's direction, "Hey, doofus, get over here!"

I can still feel the sting. Most of us have been called names like that, and worse. But to hear it from your dad and with your teammates looking on . . .

I didn't go over and punch him like I wanted to, but after that our coaches doubled down. We agreed that where Matt was concerned, our job was to build him up. We would let him know that we believed he had what it takes, that we were proud of him, that we loved his character. He was important to the team. He mattered. He was NOT a doofus.

There's some Matt in all of us. We began searching for approval at a young age, hoping to find it at home, wondering, *What do Mom and Dad think of me? What do my siblings think of me? Am I loved here?*

Dads are the key players. I can't say enough about the importance of dads and the place they have in the hearts of their kids. The young man or young lady who knows that dad loves them and values them is miles down the road toward becoming an adult of high character and confidence. These kids have their identity planted in healthy life-giving soil.

As we age our hunting ground expands beyond the family circle. More people matter to us, and we wonder if we matter to them: friends, teachers, coaches, band leaders, and girls. Eventually we start looking to our boss, colleagues, neighbors, spouse, and even our children. Since we perceive ourselves largely through the eyes of others, we always want to know who loves us and why.

> My self-perception should come through the Lord's eyes, not through the eyes of others.

Like I said, most of us *start* looking for approval at home. Some are fortunate to find it there. Others, like Matt, don't. Often other men—grandfathers, uncles, coaches, mentors, and even older brothers—need to step into the gap. Throughout life, as we move into education, jobs, professional training, career, and marriage, we can benefit from the approval, affirmations, and guidance of other men who have traveled more miles than we have.

GOOD JEFF, BAD JEFF

Bill Walsh was the head coach of the San Francisco 49ers when I played for them in 1986. He was a great once-in-a-lifetime coach, able to make his players better by helping them see themselves as more skilled than they thought they were. That may sound ludicrous in the world of professional football where gargantuan egos are often on display, but the truth is that people who are on top of their game are often still on the approval hunt and plagued by self-doubt. I know I was.

Coach Walsh sometimes held private coaching sessions with his starters. In my sessions we watched a collection of "Good Jeff" plays and then "Bad Jeff" plays from the game film. We'd sit together as he analyzed my play, pointing out intricate details of what I did well before thoroughly coaching me on what I could improve. The most powerful thing in Bill's approach was that he defined me by "Good Jeff," by my strengths. He didn't ignore "Bad Jeff"; he just didn't let those bad plays define me. He called me up into my higher capability.

Some years later, I better understood how elevating that time with Coach Walsh had been. Because he coached me as if I were already the better player that I would later become, I stepped up my game—in execution and leadership. Coach Walsh believed and saw me at a higher level than I'd seen. His approval and high expectations invited me up. I began to play at a higher level. I started working for and expecting excellence, not just winning and avoiding failure. Big difference.

Some of us, like young Matt, have been hearing "Hey, Doofus," and repeating it to ourselves since we were boys. We need something radical, something that goes to the root, something that grabs us by our soul.

THE GIDEON PRINCIPLE—CALLING UP GOOD MEN

Imagine you're a guy who didn't have a dad around. You're six feet, three inches tall, strong on the outside, wounded on the inside. You're angry. You drink hard. You've been in some brawls and spent a few nights in jail. But you're a good carpenter, so your boss takes a chance on you and promotes you to foreman on a high-dollar house build.

You work hard, bring your best to the job every day, and lead your crew well. You complete the job on time, and the boss is impressed. He comes to the job site for the final inspection. It's his reputation on the line, and because a satisfied client is the best marketing there is in the world of residential construction, he takes these inspections seriously. When he's done, he nods approvingly, and says, "Great job! Came in on time, fabulous craftsmanship, solid leadership of the team. Thank you!"

Then, he does something unexpected. He grasps your shoulders, looks you in the eye and says, "Chuck, you're a good man."

This isn't a parable. It really happened. The builder's name is Don and his first-time foreman's name is Chuck. When Don called Chuck a good man, it was more than Chuck could handle. He sniffled, then teared up, and then sobbed. Before he knew it, he was in Don's embrace, a man half a foot shorter than he was, and the first one to ever affirm him and name him a good man.

I might have teared up a bit too when Don told me this story.

The fact is, when Don spoke those words to him, Chuck *wasn't* a good man. Not yet. He was a good builder, but the good man part? That was just getting started. But it did start, and it continued—because a good man named Don believed in Chuck and called him up.

Chuck had a yearning to be a good man and Don knew how to look deep and draw it out. He saw the character in Chuck that others hadn't seen—the desire to do well, to live responsibly, to work hard, and to lead with humility. Don identified those things in Chuck and saw the man he could become rather than the man he had been.

GIDEON: A MAN IN THE MAKING

The same thing happened to a guy who lived a few thousand years ago. His name was Gideon. His story is told in Judges 6.

During a seven-year period of spiritual darkness and widespread fear, a young man named Gideon was trying to keep his head down. Day in and day out, he and his neighbors lived with the anxiety of knowing they could be attacked at any moment.

Gideon seemed to be a decent guy. When we first come across him, he's doing his best to keep his family fed and hidden. He was also hiding. He was not a man of courage or leadership. He was subsisting, doing his work in the confines of a wine vat that should have been done in the open air.

Gideon didn't expect much from himself, and he was certain that nobody else did either. He described his family as the weakest in the territory and himself was the youngest in his family. Gideon saw himself as the least of the least.

It's in this moment of hiding and obscurity that God breaks into Gideon's story. This is when Gideon receives his identity, his manhood and his mission.

God dispatches His angel with a message for Gideon. Listen to this greeting: "Gideon, The Lord is with you, great warrior, mighty man of valor."

Did you hear that? *Great warrior. Mighty man of valor.*

That's not at all who Gideon was. Not yet, anyway.

But God sees the future and He names Gideon according to what he will become rather than what he is. God speaks Gideon's identity and destiny into him, and by receiving this identity, everything about Gideon changes. Sure, he still has some doubts and needs reassurances from God on more than one occasion, but he did in fact become a great leader—on a national scale. He ends up governing Israel for over forty years.

> Believing what God says about me will lead me to become the man He has called me to be.

YOUR TURN

I call what Don did for Chuck and what Coach Walsh did for me "The Gideon Principle." It's not reserved for a few choice guys. It's for you too.

God sees the good in you that He created. He willingly gifted His forgiveness and reconciling perfection to you through Jesus. He already sees the ways you will transform when you hand control of your life over to Him. He sees the version of you that He intended all along.

You may not see that version of yourself very well, if at all. And you really can't see it if you have not received Father God's welcome back invitation to be adopted into His family.

If you're like most guys, no matter what front you're putting up, you're looking at the uncertain and fearful version of yourself. Beating yourself up, slouching in the corner with the stench of shame suffocating you. Shields up, making sure nobody gets a hint of "the real you."

> My identity is not a self-improvement project, but the gift of a loving heavenly Father whose approval does not need to be earned.

But that's *not* the real you, not the way God looks on you. He sees you as who He can free you to become.

Are you beyond self-improvement? Yes. We all are. We simply cannot fix all that needs fixing. But God can. We are not beyond His care or His reach. God is an awesome Father and He sent Jesus to be our solution, to rescue, adopt, and equip us. It depends upon His character and goodness, not ours. *He* makes us men. We don't do this ourselves. We receive it from Him. He gives us His goodness.

We are not the sum total of our failures and flaws. Our identity is not locked to our past or bound up in the mess we carry hidden on the inside or stuck to the veneered image we display on the outside. True identity comes from the perfect Father who paid the highest price to bring us back to Himself.

Remember, it wasn't a coach, boss, or even his dad that approached Gideon in such a transformative way. It was God personally. And Father God wants to relate to you and me in the same way. He wants us to know that we don't have to *earn* His approval. He'll give it to us. We just need to receive it.

ASK MYSELF

- "On a 1 to 10 scale from confused to crystal clear, how secure am I in my identity—who I really am apart from any image or variable measures?"

MY ACTIONS

- I'll seek proof that "God gives us His goodness" by reading & paraphrasing 2 Corinthians 5:17-21 and Romans 5:8.
- I will seek to find a man who is most likely to see my true value and potential as God sees me. I will ask if I can spend some time together with him.
- I will practice the Gideon Principle on someone else. I will speak value and confidence into a young guy with my life.

"Now, with God's help, I shall become myself."

—**Sören Kierkegaard**

"The Christian Gospel is that I am so flawed that Jesus had to die for me, yet I am so loved and valued that Jesus was glad to die for me. This leads to deep humility and deep confidence at the same time. It undermines both swaggering and sniveling. I cannot feel superior to anyone, and yet I have nothing to prove to anyone. I do not think more of myself nor less of myself. Instead, I think of myself less."

—**Timothy Keller**

6

BE RE-FATHERED

Ed never met his biological dad. His father was a navy pilot who died before Ed was born. Ed's mom then married another navy pilot, who, as you might expect, raised him with a rigid, military discipline. There was plenty of friction between them, but also some good times and helpful life preparation.

Steve fared worse in the Dad Department. His dad abandoned the family when Steve was just six years old.

Your dad may have had mostly negative words for you, or you never really felt his approval. Or maybe he spoke too few words to you to make you confident in your identity. Maybe you were fortunate enough to grow up with a dad who affirmed you with his words. But no matter where your dad falls on the awful-to-great scale, none of us had perfect dads.

THE NEED FOR A PERFECT FATHER

As for me, I had a pretty amazing dad. He was with us and was super affectionate and encouraging. He loved our family well. But he was not perfect, and I needed a perfect dad.

So did Ed, and so did Steve. And so do you. We all need a perfect father.

Our father is the main source of our identity. His presence, character, and approval deeply matter to us. We are especially shaped by his words— by curses and blessings—and even by his silence. Our dad's words are imprinted on us, for good or for harm.

Words are important because they answer our questions.

> "Words kill, words give life; they're either poison or fruit—you choose." (Proverbs 18:21 The Message)

Every boy has questions for his dad. Some are about life skills and relationships. Some questions change and grow as boys change and grow. Then there are the questions we might not voice but we desperately want answered from our dads. John Eldredge identified those big questions:

- Do I measure up?
- Do I have what it takes?
- What is my purpose?
- Am I a man?

It's expecting a lot for a dad to answer them well and completely, especially as an imperfect man who was raised by another imperfect man.

Without answers, we spend our life looking for a clear identity, a durable sense of belonging, and a way to know what our purpose in life is and how to pursue it. We're trapped in our insecurities, pride, and selfish destructive ways.

In fact, we need more than that. We need answers to the questions we're not asking, and we need to be prepared for anything life can throw at us.

So, I repeat, we all *need* a perfect dad.

Which is why God wants to re-Father us.

Bottom line: young guys, and many older guys, are all looking for a father's help. Whether they know it or not, what they're really looking for is a relationship with God—as He really is, not as we imagine Him.

THE PERFECT FATHER

Let's face it: A huge problem is that God is under-represented by even the best dads and badly represented by the absent, abusive, neglectful or emotionally distant dads. To even *want* a relationship with this perfect Father, we'll need to open our minds to put aside many negative feelings and inaccurate thoughts about Him.

I invite you to try a reset with the Heavenly Father. Throw out the impressions and ideas you've picked up. Start fresh. Ask Him who He really is and consider Him anew. He is so much better and gracious than we've presumed or imagined Him to be. He's not like the pictures painted in our culture. He's not who "religion" has often portrayed Him to be.

To describe the many aspects of Father God's goodness and perfection would take a much longer book—written by a much smarter guy. But I'll say this: The perfect Father proved His perfection through His perfect love. He gave His perfect Son to die the death we deserved and take the punishment for our rebellion.

He did that to bring us back as His sons and create an eternal paradise that will make everything wrong on earth right and everything good even better. Our Father God's perfect Son Jesus showed us what our Father is like.

Jesus told a story that painted a vivid and powerful picture of our Heavenly Father. You can read the story in Chapter 15 of the book of Luke. As you read, put yourself in the place of the two very different sons who had disconnected from their father in different ways.

> I need to be re-Fathered by my perfect Father God who loves me.

The impulsive, greedy, and pleasure-dominated younger son took his inheritance and ran. The rule-following, moralistic and stingy older son stayed, but his heart was filled with comparison and contempt. The father was an amazing forgiver, a generous dad who embraced his sons unconditionally, even throwing a party for the runaway son after he returned.

That's the kind of Father you have.

To be re-Fathered begins by accepting God's invitation to come back to Him and be forgiven and adopted as His son—with all the favor, rights, and privileges.

ED

I mentioned earlier that my friend, Ed, was raised by a high-performing stepdad who was a Navy pilot and pilot trainer. It's no surprise that this man carried his military ways into his parenting. As a result, Ed grew up to be a performance-driven overcomer. He gutted through rehab from injuries that could have ended his football career and went on to play offensive line in the NFL for three years with the Jets, Giants and Rams.

Ed became an *on-fire-for-Jesus* guy in college and carried that same spiritual intensity into his NFL and post-NFL days, eventually becoming a pastor and fatherhood leader. I remember waiting for my turn to speak after him at an event with him when I was a young quarterback with the LA Rams. I was feeling jealous of and intimidated by his bold speaking ability. He seemed to have so much more confidence, knowledge of the Bible, and passion than I did.

You may not have picked up on it, but Ed still didn't have his boyhood questions answered at that time. He'd missed a vital aspect of fathering when he was a boy, and he carried those gaps into adulthood. NFL and ministry success were not enough. The high-octane work ethic, infectious confidence, encyclopedic knowledge of the Bible, and persuasive communication skills combined weren't enough to fill the void. These are things that only one Father can fill to the full, but an earthly dad can get it started—even an imperfect one. But like many men, Ed hadn't gotten that start.

At 40, Ed was a success, but he didn't have peace or give it to his wife and daughters. He was still trying to earn his identity. He was stuck in a performance-based life—as a son, a pro football player, a pastor, speaker, husband, dad, and Christian. But his performance approach couldn't nurture hearts. It wasn't translating into success in his relationships with his wife and daughters. He seemed to be on a treadmill that never let him catch up or relax. It was all too much, yet it wasn't enough. He hit a wall.

He went on a quest to really know his perfect Father. He discovered a Father who took great pleasure in him and wanted to re-Father him.

Ed's life, including his faith journey, marriage, parenting, and ministry radically changed. The process began with Ed asking God questions like:

Why do I feel like a "less than"?

How do You feel about me?

Can You change me?

What am I holding onto that prevents me from experiencing You?

What lies have I believed about myself and about You?

What do You plan for me after I die?

How do I come to you?

What do you want to say to me?

How can I hear from you?

Can you help me better love my wife and kids?

Ed began listening to his Father expectantly, reading the Bible as a son (not a "Christian"), and talking to others whom he thought could help him. The answers that eventually came set Ed free. He was able to forgive and let go of the past. He dropped the bondage of insecurity and performance. He stopped image-building and trying so hard to be liked. He stopped pushing, controlling and stressing over results, which made his home life much happier.

In a nutshell, Ed was set free from trying to earn his identity once he realized that he could simply receive it from his Father.

That's what being re-Fathered can do for all of us.

Ed now says, "*When you enter into this relationship with the Father through His Son Jesus, He'll bring you all that you were meant to be and want to be. It comes as a gift He offers when you accept relationship and identity as the Father's son.*"

No matter what our culture and tweaked versions of Christianity imply, God offers so much more than a crisis hotline or lifeline to avoid Hell. God is a loving Father in every situation.

Your journey can change. Your story can transform. Your identity can become clear. You can live with purpose, mission and calling.

The reality is we are created in the image of a magnificent loving Father who knew from the start that we'd try to go out on our own only to end up drifting far away from Him. He knew we'd have lots of questions and that we'd mostly look for the answers in unhelpful places.

Being re-Fathered means receiving my identity from the Father, not earning it.

But—God invites us back. He paid the debt we'd run up and took on the death sentence we'd incurred for rejecting Him. We cannot fathom the sacrifice He gave to bring us back. Saul of Tarsus, whom Jesus renamed Paul, was a man who knew as well as any man what it meant to be re-Fathered. He explains that God initiates love and then loves unconditionally like this, "But God demonstrates His own love toward us, in that while we were still sinners, Christ died for us." (Romans 5:8 NASB).

Nobody loves you, likes you, values you, and yearns for you like Father God does. Nobody can.

Despite the trauma and failures of our past, God does not want us to live as victims or walk on in defeat. He calls and empowers us to be overcomers. By His grace, we are "more than conquerors through [Jesus] who loved us" (Romans 8:39).

I encourage you to take a week, or a month, to read and wrestle with what the perfect Father and His Son say to us in the Amplified or New Living Translation of Paul's letter of Romans, chapter 5 and chapter 8. It explains our problem and how Jesus solves it. It tells about the new life we gain when God re-Fathers us. It explains how God knew us, chose us to be His sons and invites us into His good purpose for our lives—a greater good than we can imagine. Finally, it reminds us that no damage from the past, no attack in the present, and no trial in the future can separate us from the love of God.

The news gets even better. When you meet Him and enter this re-Fathering relationship with God, you're just getting started. Living as His well-loved son isn't something we graduate from. We grow in it and become more dependent on and confident in our Father. That's the way Jesus lived.

RE-FATHERING AND THE GIDEON PRINCIPLE

Remember our discussion about Gideon in the last chapter? He was a young man with huge challenges, opponents, doubts and fears. He didn't come from much, didn't have much going for him and didn't see much of a future. Yet, like you and me, he was meant to be a courageous leader.

Have you ever felt like he felt at the beginning of that story? Afraid and living in the shadows, just trying to scrape together a bit of food for his family. He doesn't really know who he is.

When God re-Fathers him, He gives Gideon his new identity, worth and character. He still had questions, but now he knew who to ask and depend on.

God wants to do the same for you—to name you and give you a destiny and purpose. There is no greater calling—no greater identity to live up to—than to be His son.

SEE IT IN ACTION

Marvin Charles didn't have his dad or mom in his life. When he did find out who his dad was, he was the exact opposite of healthy. Marvin had been molested and sexualized at a young age and slid into an illicit street life. Then prison, drug treatment and having a few children led him to Jesus. He wanted a different life for himself and his four kids than he'd had on the streets.

"Part of my transition back into the community happened because I hit the wall and went into treatment," Marvin says. "I received Jesus as my Savior and Lord, and I got baptized in treatment. My relationship with Jesus was a new thing. I was all in. I'd been a general in Satan's army and I committed to being just as faithful and committed to Jesus as I was to the life Satan had me in. I'd have held up a bank with two 45s if Satan had told me, so I took the same approach to God. I got deeply engaged in the urban center black church community."

"I was a minister aiming to save others, but after 10 years or so, I felt a pull for something more real, something better." Marvin explains, "I felt the Holy Spirit pulling me to something freer. I entered a relationship with a couple of white guys that really impacted my life. They didn't put Jesus in a box. They just set him in my lap. I got really interested. I wanted to know more about this freedom—this freedom in Christ."

Marvin was being drawn to being re-Fathered by God—and he was about to have his "Gideon" moment.

"One of these men came to my home. He stood me up and put his hands on my shoulders. He looked me in the eyes and said . . .

'Marvin, you are my beloved son in whom I am well pleased.'

'WHY DID YOU DO THAT?' I asked.

'Because you have never been **validated**. I want to validate you and I want you to know that Jesus validates you.'

"I called both my sons, young teenagers at the time, out of the bedroom and I immediately did the same thing for them. I validated them. I told the guys, 'If I had to wait until I was forty-five to receive this validation, how much more do I need to do this right this moment for my sons?'"

Marvin continued, "If they thought enough of me to do this for me, I wanted to think enough of my sons to do it for them. This was **my transition to manhood**. I began to follow this relationship pattern. These men treated relationships so powerfully. They were showing me things that are influencing me to this day."

"This was a huge leap in my transformation as a man, father and mentor to other fatherless men like me."

In just a matter of minutes, Marvin had experienced the Gideon Principle—and then he gave it to his sons. He'd also begun a new re-Fathering relationship with God.*

---

* Marvin is my deeply valued friend. He's a remarkable leader alongside his amazing wife, Jeanett. He's been mentoring men ever since he was befriended, mentored and re-Fathered. Their ministry, Divine Alternatives for Dads Services, has mentored over 4,000 disconnected dads in manhood, fatherhood, and engagement with their children. Learn more at www.aboutdads.org.

ASK MYSELF

- "Deep down, what do I fear and worry about that impacts how I pursue validation?"
- "What do I yearn for, seek and count on to be OK and feel good about myself?"
- "Have I received my identity as Father God's son along with His blessing?"
- "Have I given this blessing to my children, grandchildren or a young guy who needs it from me?"

MY ACTIONS

- I will step away from work, screens, and all my tasks for 30-60 minutes. I will take a walk in a peaceful place. I will listen to my heart. If I desire to be validated in my identity, I will ask Father God to begin re-Fathering me.
- I'll read Luke 3:22 to discover what Jesus experienced after his cousin John baptized Him. Specifically, I'll look for how Almighty God the Father named and blessed and delighted in Jesus. I'll envision myself being the one coming out of the water to hear my Father define and bless me.
- I'll read Luke 9:25 and Matthew 17:5 to envision the Father blessing Jesus in the presence of His three closest friends. I'll notice how Abba Father affirmed Jesus' identity as a Son; confirmed His love for Jesus; stated His pleasure in Jesus; and reinforced Jesus as "My Chosen One".
- I'll turn to 2 Corinthians 5:21 to grasp and receive what the Father and Jesus give me. It's this: we who sin get credit for the righteousness of Christ. We're made righteous in God's eyes because Jesus who never sinned took sin's punishment for us. To receive this reality is to be adopted and fully accepted as God's beloved son.

"The Father is pursuing you. He is asking, 'Son, are you ready to become who you were born to be? We can finish this together.'"

—**Morgan Snyder**

Be re-Fathered, not un-fathered.

7

THE RECEIVE PRINCIPLE

My former teammates Jerry Rice and Steve Largent own these fashion-challenged but universally esteemed yellow sports jackets. They earned them as members of the Pro Football Hall of Fame. A small portion of the many passes and touchdown receptions in their career came from me. I was lucky enough to witness the focus and enthusiasm with which they received every single pass.

Notice that I said 'received' instead of 'caught.'

We've all seen a player catch a pass only for the opponent to knock it out of his hands. It wasn't a reception. He only caught it temporarily.

But a great receiver eyes the ball in with intense focus. He snags the ball and immediately tucks it into his body with a safe grip, smothering its tips with his hand and armpit. *Receiving* is done with focus, intensity and the sustained priority of possessing the ball.

CONNECTING WITH THE FATHER

Jesus lived by the Receive Principle. His constant priority was to connect to His Father and receive His identity and purpose from Him. He got alone. He listened. He prayed. He waited. He thanked. He depended. He expected. He asked for help. He told people that His Father was always working and so was He. He only did and said what He received from His Father. He and His Father were one.

That is the type of relationship God wants for each of us, as His sons.

If you hang around people who truly follow Jesus, you'll hear them talk about "faith." Faith is the basis for how we relate to God. It's our confidence that God will do everything He has promised to do and give everything He has promised to give.

> Receiving from God is not passive, but an active welcoming of the identity He has given me.

Why faith? Because if we could see Him or hear His voice out loud, if He explained every detail and answered every question and prayer immediately, it would no longer require faith. It would take no trust, and that's what God looks for in His sons and daughters.

Even so, we need to put ourselves in the position to receive what God wants us to have from Him. Receiving is not passive or optional. And like any wide receiver will tell you, it's much easier said than done. Receiving from God may not seem "easy" for us, but achieving identity, significance and peace on our own is impossible.

It's the central principle of real and good manhood. Society convinces us that life is performing, achieving, and earning. In reality, life itself is received from the Creator. All good originates from God, so absolutely anything of value and goodness starts with Him, not us. Jesus lived this way. If it was the way for Him, how much more do you and I need to live by receiving continually from the Father?

RECEIVING LIKE GIDEON

Remember where Gideon was before God called him to lead His people. He was living in fear, working cautiously to avoid getting robbed or attacked. Suddenly, Gideon's story becomes epic, not because of what he does—because of what someone else does with him.

Remember, God calls him "a mighty man of valor," an identity that's totally new to the man hiding in a hole.

God sees the whole movie, not just the single frame. He was letting Gideon know what kind of man he would become. He was declaring Gideon's character, far before he had it. If you fast-forward through Gideon's story, he does indeed live up to that greeting. Before it was all over, Gideon would be a military leader and national hero.

What does Gideon's story have to do with you and me?

In the previous chapters, we've been talking about identity, about who you really are—not who you've been condemned and shamed into being. This was Gideon's awakening, the receiving of his true identity. The identity God wanted him to embrace.

RECEIVING AND RE-FATHERING

This was a re-Fathering moment for Gideon. The Perfect Father was calling him into a relationship that would forever change him—not because Gideon had proven himself or earned it but because of God and His nature as a good and perfect Father.

A WHOLE NEW WAY OF LIVING

Re-Fathering is much more than a momentary experience, however. It is a whole new way of living as God's son. God doesn't drop in, give us a new name and identity, and then leave. He sticks around. He stays with us—forever. We don't graduate, get a diploma and move on as a man on our own. We learn to live as a son. He continues to mature and transform us as He leads us to grow and fulfill our purpose.

In Chapter 3 and Chapter 6, we talked about the birth of our relationship with God. Receiving God as your Father is every day that comes after. The rest of our lives is a journey of growth and the adventure of living as a son of the perfect Father.

For now, you might still be seeing only the pre-valor version of yourself, the guy who's still threshing wheat in a winepress. Your ego is brittle, your confidence is AWOL. Maybe you're still beating yourself up over the past, hanging on to shame and desperate to prove yourself.

God sees you like He saw Gideon—beyond your past and present, to your future. He sees the image of Himself that He created in you. He's calling you up not for who you've been but for who He's going to make you. "*The Lord is with you, O mighty man of valor.*"

WHAT GOD WANTS TO GIVE YOU

During the blitz (trouble and opportunity) of COVID-19, all my speaking events canceled. I had more time to write. I asked God to lead me into a season of being re-Fathered. He reshaped me as I dug into the Bible and Dave Patty's book, *Father God: Daring to Draw Near.* I read Father God's affirmation of Jesus at His baptism and transfiguration. It connects to us because of truth in 2 Corinthians 5:21, "For God made Christ, who never sinned, to be the offering for our sin, so that we could be made right with God through Christ (NLT)." Our eternal Father credits us with Jesus' righteousness. He remakes us, adopts us, and affirms us. As He affirmed Jesus, "You are My Son, My Beloved, in You I am well-pleased *and* delighted! . . . My Chosen One." (Luke 3:22; Luke 9:35 AMP).

Dave Patty studied the relationship between God the Father and Jesus the Son in the Bible. He writes about four "gifts" Jesus the Son received from God the Father: (1) identity, (2) love, (3) pleasure—the Father's approval, and (4) place—one's purpose and belonging. Dave began to see how each of these gifts meets the needs that all men have:

1. *Identity* gives value.
2. *Love* brings security.
3. *Pleasure and Approval* give energy and motivation.
4. *Place* brings honor.

Our Father is a giver. As the son of this perfect Father, you'll spend the rest of your life receiving from Him. Believe me, He has plenty He wants to give you. Here are some of the vital things He gives:

1. An accurate, unspoiled view of Himself
2. A true understanding of how He sees you and feels about you
3. The blueprint of His perfect Father-Son relationship with Jesus that he desires for you
4. Freedom from sin's control and shame from your past
5. Experiencing how prayer works
6. Understanding, appreciation, and enthusiasm for what the Bible teaches
7. Feeling His unconditional pleasure, approval and delight in you, particularly when you trust Him and express the abilities He's given you
8. The courage to face your fears, failures, secrets, risks, doubts and worries
9. Healing from the wounds you've received
10. Forgiveness for the wounds you've caused
11. Revitalization of your true purpose, passions, and motivations
12. Embracing His desires for you—knowing they're better than your own can be
13. Release from living with lies, false narratives, and unhealthy habits

14. Release from pointless and exhausting efforts to prop up a false identity
15. The desire to trust Him with everything and all outcomes
16. Constant awareness of your secured eternity in His perfect kingdom
17. Exhilaration and confidence of God living in and guiding you with peace and wisdom to handle any situation

Remember, He *wants* to give you these blessings. He's not a reluctant father, offering them to you but not caring whether you *actually* receive them. He's not biased, either. He doesn't offer them to some super-spiritual guys only and not to all of His sons. Neither is he a demanding father, making you earn them. He's not a fickle father, giving or withholding based on His mood. He's a perfect Father—*the* Perfect Father. He gives joyfully, generously, and graciously.

> Allowing God to re-Father me involves accepting the many gifts He has for me which I cannot earn.

Sounds pretty good, huh?

But how do you receive it all?

RECEIVING EVERYTHING GOD HAS FOR YOU

These are some ways I keep receiving from God. Ask Father God to direct you and you'll find, in your own way and timing, some may help you continue being re-Fathered.

- Set up a private place to be with God—no interruptions or distractions.
- Meet Him there early. Start with 2 or 3 minutes with Him. Be consistent. If you missed it in the morning, sit with Him at night.
- Call Him *Father, Abba or Dad.* Present yourself to Him as His son. Ask to connect with Him all day long.

- Talk to Him. Listen for the thoughts and impressions He may give you.
- Invite Him to take over. Slowly pray, "Father God, Lord Jesus, Holy Spirit—Father me. Lead me. Fill me."
- Ask Him to help you receive His love—to truly experience it, accept it, embrace it.
- Ask God how He sees and feels about you. Write out Romans 5:8 and 2 Corinthians 5:21.
- Ask Him to reveal how you've been trying to earn your identity and validation. Ask Him to release you from that impossible approach.
- Ask Him to help you fully receive His gift of your identity as an adopted son—fully forgiven, accepted, and approved.
- Tell him exactly what you fear, struggle with, worry about, or need help handling.
- Ask Him to make it comfortable praying from Jesus' pattern of prayer in Matthew 6:9-13.
- Take walks to have conversations with God in the expanse of His creation.
- Ask God to prompt you on what and who to pray for. Ask His Holy Spirit to guide you.
- Write your questions to God in a journal or notes on your phone. Expect Him to answer eventually. Be patient.
- Ask Him to free you from lies you've believed and wrong interpretations of your past.
- Read the Bible as a son reading messages from your Father. Expect to hear from Him.
- Focus on things to be grateful for and thank Him.
- Pause and pray spontaneously throughout the day, alone or with someone if they're open or need it. Short. Direct. Real.
- Continually listen for God's quiet and present voice.

A PROCESS

Gideon didn't behave like a mighty man of valor overnight. The day the angel appeared to him marked the beginning of a long journey—one that brought him to the fulfillment of his destiny and purpose.

Whether your relationship with God begins today or began years ago, or even if you haven't yet said yes to Him, He is making this promise to all who come to Him through Christ: "I will never leave you nor forsake you" (Hebrews 13:5 ESV).

He's an amazing, generous and perfect Father. When you trust Him and receive from Him, you're a well-loved son, a man of valor.

It's not always easy. For a few years now, I've been intentional about relating to Father God as a son as Jesus did. I've been quiet with God more, taken more walks, asked more questions and invited his direction in every situation. I trust Him but I don't hear Him speak or guide me in obvious ways every day. Somedays, I'm tempted to be frustrated by that. But I remind myself He cares totally and is always at work.

Other days, you'll feel God's guidance and provision. Last year, I had been struggling with how to adapt my speaking fees to the realities of Covid. At that point, all my events were done over Zoom. One night, I suggested a fee arrangement with a men's event leader that was likely more than what they were prepared for. I didn't like how I felt after the call ended.

The next morning, I talked it over with God on an early walk and came back for my weekly huddle call over Zoom with three friends. Each of us shared the most important thing in our life and let another pray for us. I mentioned my angst from the night before. When I finished, David chimed in, "Man, Jeff, I've been in your shoes. Can I share something with you? You are a steward of opportunities God gives you. Your message and communication ability are gifts from God, and so is each invitation to speak. Don't worry about fees and money. If you're available and supposed to accept an invitation, give it your best with your whole heart, and leave all the results and getting paid up to God. He more than takes care of all that in the long run."

As he was speaking, I experienced the Receive Principle. I could feel God speaking to me, recalibrating me and setting me free from the financial focus, ambition and negotiation. He was showing me how to handle it.

Today, I can vividly remember that experience of receiving. I remind myself of it so I'll stay tuned in and ready to receive guidance from God.

Receiving is about staying alert to God like a young son to his father. He can speak through the Bible, as a voice in your head when you pray, through clear thoughts He gives you, through a mentor or friend, devotion, podcast, sermon or book. Sometimes, He speaks through one circumstance shutting down and another opening up. Over the two-year Covid era, it's been awesome to relax and see God provide for me in totally different channels than live speaking. I just needed to remember that He is smarter and kinder to me than I am to myself. Trust, relax and listen for His message to you.

HOW CAN I DO THIS?

I pray that the message of this book is God's message to you. Since I'm imperfect, I'm sure the book is imperfect. But I trust God to use it to give you His very best answer to all your questions and guidance for being the man you were created to be.

Ready for the bad news?

You aren't a real or a good man. You can't be totally real and completely good.

Now here's the great news. Only one man was and is—Jesus. As God Himself, Jesus took on human form. He lived in a complete and constant relationship with His Father God. Everything He was and did on earth, He received from His Father. He showed us the way to be ourselves. He showed us the way to live here and now. And He showed us the way we can live with God forever after our short life on this earth is over.

Being the man we want to be, the man God designed us to be, depends on accepting not just the bad and great news above. It depends on how we respond to the worst and best news.

The worst news: God created humanity to relate to Him, enjoy and glorify Him while sharing steward-ship under His benevolent reign. But the angel Lucifer chose not to live in harmony with Him. He rebelled and became God's enemy. From Adam and Eve forward, humanity has also disconnected from God and gone its own way.

> The gospel contains both the worst and the best news.

Here's the best news: God already began his plans to correct and restore it all. He has gone to great lengths to communicate with us humans. Everything written from every prophet and apostle in the Bible points to Jesus. Jesus' words to us, along with His death and resurrection, encompass the full message from God to us.

So, how will you respond to the worst and best news, which is the tragic and triumphant universal story in which we all exist? More specif-ically, how will you and I respond to its central figure?

From this day forward, we can live by receiving from our Father through Christ, His Spirit and scripture. We receive our salvation which brings forgiveness and eternal life. We receive our identity as His adopted sons. We receive our WHY: our place, purpose, mission and calling as God's representatives in every place and situation. We receive His power to do as He leads when we humble ourselves, admit our weakness and confess our sins. We receive minute-to-minute guidance from our Father if we turn to Him and His Word like Jesus did.

ASK MYSELF

- "What big lie do I believe about myself?"
- "Regardless of any or no validation by my father, have I received Father God's adoption and blessing as His son which come through receiving Jesus as my Savior, Lord and greatest friend?"

MY ACTION

- I will begin each day as a son receiving my identity and God's presence: "Father God, Lord Jesus, Holy Spirit—Thank you that You chose me as Your son. Father me. Lead me. Fill me."
- I will go to the scriptures in the My Action section of Chapter 6 and align them with the four gifts Father God gives to the heart of a man which Dave Patty describes. I'll ask God to help me fully receive them: assurance of my identity as a son, God's love, God's pleasure, and my place (purpose and belonging).

"Grace is not opposed to effort; it is opposed to earning."
—Dallas Willard

"God shapes the world by prayer. Prayer is not the foe to work, it does not paralyze activity. It works mightily; prayer itself is the greatest work."
—E. M. Bounds

Replace DO & EARN with RECEIVE & BE.

8

THE ESSENCE OF MANHOOD

In the last chapter, we talked about Jesus as the ultimate man and solution. Now, let's look to Him as the model for manhood.

First, we must know the real Jesus—which isn't automatic. For 2,000 years, he's changed history, civilizations, and millions of people. But 2,000 years have allowed for a lot of forgetting, redefining and reinterpreting. For centuries, he's been denied, religion-ized, reformed, repackaged, misunderstood, and ignored.

THE REAL JESUS

We all interpret. But we have to stick to the facts. He wasn't a white dude. He wasn't a black dude. Although He was a faithful Jew, Jesus wasn't a religious hypocrite or a political figure. Jesus was the only man who was and is completely real and perfectly good.

I'm not going to get things perfect. But my aim is to help you get a better view and understanding of how Jesus lived as a man. Not just for the sake of knowing or being inspired, but for living your life.

> By knowing Jesus and living like Him, I live out a masculinity that is real and good.

His purpose was to show us His Father and bring us back to Him. By knowing Jesus and living like Him, we live out a masculinity that is real and good. By good, I don't mean flawless, fixed-up or morally perfect. Only Jesus was that. Good means positive, unselfish and beneficial toward others. Good makes situations, places, relationships and groups better than before.

To know the real Jesus, we must be real with ourselves and face reality. Face those deeper questions, the ones that might be gnawing in your gut. They need to be surfaced or else you won't fully meet the real Jesus. Questions like:

- What is Truth?
- What does a Perfect Father look like?
- Is God real? Where is He? Why don't I sense or feel Him?
- Is Jesus a man or God? How can He be both?
- Is it true Jesus fulfilled every prophecy made about Him?
- Is it true that hundreds of people saw Him alive again (after His crucifixion), before He returned forty days later to His Father in Heaven?
- Why do some high-profile "Christian" figures and some people who label themselves "Christians" live so differently than Jesus? Why is there so much hypocrisy and ugliness in "Christians" and "Christianity"?
- Why is oppression, prejudice, racism, injustice, evil, denial, and defensiveness so pervasive? Why is power blind or uncaring of the way it marginalizes people without power or those who challenge the status quo? Where's justice?

- What should I feel because Jesus was crucified? Shame, guilt, forgiveness, gratitude?
- Was Jesus a victim of death by crucifixion? Or did He choose to allow it?
- Is eternity real? What is it like? Will I need forgiveness to enter heaven? If so, how do I get it?
- How do I find satisfaction, peace and real joy—something that will last?
- If God has a plan for me, when and how will I know it? Why am I flopping around?
- Is this "Christian faith" viable? Does it work? Or is it strict, boring and impractical? Could I be missing the true essence of faith?
- What is the key to actually thriving and overcoming life's mess?
- How good is what God wants for me? Can I depend on that? Why don't I?

I'd love to discuss these questions over some long meals. If you want the best answers, you can ask God directly and be serious in seeking His answers through His Word.

That's what my football buddy Ed McGlasson started doing when he sought to be re-Fathered by God at age 40. He went directly to the source, reading the book God gave us. I recommend you write down all your doubts and questions. Also ask your questions of a mature, solid believer or a pastor. You might be surprised by the answers God gives you.

Many of our confusions, frustrations and problems with Jesus are from self-crafted or societal interpretations of God and Jesus. Usually, it's based on narratives from certain people, leaders, groups, or churches. Those are faulty examples because they're usually not following a reliably accurate version of Jesus and His way.

Man-made religion and modern self-centered consumerism have pulled away from Jesus as the epicenter and from the grace of his sacrificial death. Or they've watered it down with a me-centric, comfort-oriented, eternity-forgetting version of faith.

Want to know and experience the real Jesus and Father? First, let Him off the hook for the false imitations and their counterfeit solutions. God already predicted and proved His solution to humanity's universal problem of rebellious separation and the brokenness of sin, evil and death.

Fakes and counterfeits? Yep, Jesus even said that when He ushers in His eternal kingdom's paradise of heaven, He will tell many to depart— because, despite the ways they advertised themselves and threw His name around—He'll tell them He never knew them because they never received and gave themselves to Him (Matthew 7:21-23).

You know how messed up messages and perceptions can get when we rely on Twitter, Facebook posts and texts. It's like the game of *Telephone*. Read the Bible for yourself and get some help studying it for answers to your key questions. Give God the benefit of the doubt. Suspending your skepticism or disappointment with Him may help you realize you were thrown off by bad advertising. Allow Him to reach you directly.

What has Jesus made abundantly clear? He is God, the very word of God and the promised Messiah. The Bible chronicles humanity's need for Him, His life, His mission, His teaching, His crucifixion, His resurrection, His future return, and His eternal reign in a kingdom that was initiated here on earth but is to be fulfilled in eternity. Within that identity, he was the ultimate man—real and good.

Remember how I said you'd need to face the facts? Here are some more: You are valuable in God's eyes. You are also flawed beyond your own ability to repair or overcome. You know things need improving— more than a tune-up or new paint. You need transformation. *All* men need transformation.

Transformation is a change of heart and mindset that comes from God. A godly life was modeled and made possible by Jesus and He offers transformation to us.

Let's ask: *How can He be my role model and more? How can Jesus make me the very best version of myself, as God intended?*

Can I do this?

Quick answer: No. You and I can't.

Lifelong answer: Yes. God can do this in you. Your part is to trust, commit to Him and let Him take over. Surrender to someone perfect who can make transformation happen in you. He shows the way and fuels you on the journey.

JESUS' MODEL

Even Jesus, God Himself on earth, didn't live His life on his own. Jesus humbly depended on His Father in Heaven every step of the way to grow up, get to know His Father's scriptures, embrace His life mission, resist the most intense temptations the devil has ever thrown at a man, mentor a group of 12 flawed working men into friends who would change the world, perform hundreds of miracles. He relied on His Father to face the most shocking rejections, betrayals, slander, abandonment, unjust conviction, scourging and crucifixion.

He explained to His disciples that He was totally dependent on the Father. "The Son can do nothing by Himself; He can only do what He sees His Father doing. Whatever the Father does, the Son also does." (John 5:19 NLT).

The Miracle of the Loaves and Fishes is a dynamic example. You might be asking: *How am I supposed to replicate that?*

Remember, when it all started, He was pulling His men aside to connect with the Father to rest and recharge. You can do that. Earlier in this chapter, we talked about reconnecting with the Father and relying on men in your life to help.

Next, when the crowd followed them, Jesus looked up and asked His Father for the plan. You can do that. He received His plan to seat the

5,000 in groups of 50. They huddled up as Jesus relayed the play that God drew up when Jesus asked—you can do that.

He gave thanks and received God's power to feed the 5,000. You can receive power from Jesus to do things you never thought possible—to become humble to serve others.

Afterward, He went up alone into the hills to connect and receive from His Father. You can do the same.

Early that morning, Jesus walked out on the water to rescue His men in the storm-tossed boat. If you'll remember, Peter stepped out on the water while his eyes focused on Jesus. He sank when he focused on the wind, not Jesus. Like so many of us, his worry caused him to lose focus on the sustaining power source of Jesus.

But what does he do right? Sinking in the swirling waters, he calls out to Jesus. "Lord, save me!" Just like you can.

MY SWIRLING WATERS

I've had God take over and run the show when I was in deeper than I could swim. During my last season in the NFL, I experienced something rare. On the flight from Philadelphia to Houston and in all the adrenaline moments leading up to kickoff, I felt quite different than I did before the 200+ professional games I had been in. I had no confidence in how I would play. I was Jim McMahon's backup that night, but I had no idea how we'd do if I entered the game.

And yet, I felt an elevated peace that God was solidly taking care of me, no matter the outcome. The peace was amazing. But having zero confidence going into an NFL game is awkward.

How could I have no confidence in myself and still feel no fear?

Even though the stadium was packed, I was playing for an audience of one.

AUDIENCE OF ONE

I'd heard the approach to competition (and life) as a teen from the Fellowship of Christian Athletes. Practice and play to honor and please Jesus first and foremost. If you excel and win, you remain humble, and He gets the credit. If you falter and lose, Christ still loves, accepts and affirms you unconditionally.

Playing for Him sets you free—free from trying to impress a coach, peers, fans, or the media. That never summoned my best. Those audiences are always at least somewhat conditional. They're judging your performance. Playing for God, we are guaranteed His love and are then free to play relaxed, take risks and give our absolute best.

I won't get into the details of that game yet, but what I experienced afterward was wild and powerful. I'm still inconsistent. I don't always remember to live for an audience of one. My audience expands. My will replaces His

> Trusting in Jesus will give me a God-given confidence as I play and live for an audience of One.

will. My ego crowds in on His glory. My ambition overshadows His far better wise intent. My competitive streak veers off Jesus and I slip into comparing myself to others.

But it's still progressively better. That's what I want for you. We can learn and grow to live like Jesus. And yes, He will give you confidence. But it won't be self-confidence—confidence in your own track record, abilities, character, and efforts (even spiritual ones). It will be far better. It'll be God-confidence—confidence in His goodness, care, ability, and control.

Don't get me wrong. Life still happens. Circumstances don't get fixed easily. There are difficulties and tragedies. Jesus Himself prepped His friends and us—*You'll be blitzed in this world, but don't panic. I've overcome the blitz.* OK, actually He said, "In Me, you can have peace.

In this world you will have trouble. But take heart! I have overcome the world" (John 16:33 ESV).

I hear Him say it like this: *I came to give you overcoming peace. In this world you'll face trouble and blitzes. But hold on to Me for courage to overcome this world and all it throws at you. I overcame everything, including death. I turn bad things into good and dead things into life.*

Jesus had a single audience—His Father. This focused Him, defined Him and gave him fearless courage. He was devoted to His Father, His work and His way. It shaped His devotion to His friends. He invested Himself in their character, friendships and purpose. He met people's physical and spiritual hunger while staying connected to His Father constantly.

The bottom line? Living in the *Way of Jesus*, with trust in the Father's provision no matter what the outcome, gave me protection from fear and protection from the kryptonite of pride—crediting myself with success.

Losses and wins don't define me. My Father does. Failure and success don't define you. Your Father does. Suffering or comfort don't need to control us. Jesus does. He can handle anything. He can help us handle anything.

That secret is available to all of us but is found by too few. It's the key to contentment. As the Apostle Paul writes, "For I can do everything through Christ, who gives me strength." (Philippians 4:13 NLT).

> The secret to contentment is to allow myself to be defined by my heavenly Father, not by my failures or successes.

So, let's get energized—neither intimidated, nor unimpressed—by the invitation to live more like the ultimate man. The beginning is to receive Jesus into your life. He's the owner, the captain, your audience, your guide, your strength, your confidence.

To live like Jesus, we make a radical, liberating change. We shift the leadership of our life from us to Father God. We stop assuming that we are the brightest, the smartest, the wisest. We remind ourselves that God loves us, likes us and desires better for us than we can craft for ourselves. We want to know and hear what God wants for us. We live the Receive Principle, the way Jesus lived.

I asked Pat Lencioni, a foremost business teamwork expert, what's vital to being a real and good man. He said, "Roll out of bed, land on your knees and talk to God first thing every morning. I thank Him and acknowledge Him as Lord before I do anything else."

So, let's roll up our sleeves, put on our hardhat and download a brand-new operating system by walking into manhood in Jesus' shoes (sandals, cleats, boots, flip-flops . . . whatever).

Here's how Jesus received and lived real and good manhood:

FEARLESSLY FACE THE BLITZ

Jesus expected the blitz. He knew he'd be arrested, falsely accused, falsely tried, beaten, whipped and crucified as God's sacrifice for humanity's rebellion. He faced it head-on. He knew a perfect man needed to die. When we imperfect men put our pride and selfish ways to death, we revive relationships and improve outcomes. Even as He was being arrested, Jesus healed a soldier's ear that His impetuous friend Peter sliced off with his sword. Hours later, after Peter denied even knowing Jesus, Jesus was beaten, whipped, bloodied, gasping for breath and nailed to a cross. He was not vanquished or done playing offense. Jesus asked His Father to forgive the soldiers crucifying Him and the religious leaders who orchestrated it. He forgave and gave eternal life to one thief on the cross next to him who humbly turned to Jesus. He told His friend John to be a caring son to his grieving mother, Mary.

Coaching Strategy—We beat blitzes, solve conflicts, and heal divides when we are willing to die (mainly to our pride, our will, and our attempts at control). We play offense; we're not the victim or the accuser.

We deal with our own offenses, faults, and sins. We don't focus on getting even. We apologize and forgive first. We envision the long term. We're humble enough to change ourselves and focus on caring for and blessing others, *especially* when our lives are under their worst attacks. This is the key to beating blitzes.

Expect the blitz. Turn to your Father. Huddle with your team. Envision the long-term. Be humble and willing to change. Focus on blessing others.

CHAMPION THE UNDERDOG & COMEBACK

Jesus was about the underdog, the rescue and the comeback story. He loved to look for, find and rescue the lost sheep, the lost coin, the lost son. He called Himself the *Good Shepherd* and explained that good shepherds courageously risk leaving the ninety-nine safe sheep to rescue the one lost sheep. He authored this famous story illuminating His Father's character, love, and grace. The wild (prodigal) son took his inheritance, left his dad, and lived the wildlife. The arrogant, moralistic brother didn't like seeing his little brother forgiven. He was livid when their dad celebrated his brother's humble return. Jesus highlights the gracious father who loves both his sons. The dad loves the underdog and celebrates his comeback with a party. So does Jesus. He paid the debt to welcome all of us dumb, wild, arrogant guys back home. He said the last shall be first, the humble will be honored and those forgiven will love much, because of gratitude.

Coaching Strategy—We don't become real by hiding our mistakes and idiocy. We become authentic by being honest and confessing our idiocy. We don't become good men by never messing up. We become good men by admitting when we do, coming back to our heavenly Father and aiming to make life better for others. We become good men when we forgive others, celebrate someone else's turn-around and graciously open up a new future with a wife, son or friend who repents of their past. Spread the amazing grace He has shown to us.

Face our faults. Repent fully. Forgive swiftly. Support the underdog. Celebrate comebacks.

SHOW UP FOR YOUR FRIENDS

Jesus showed up for his friends. He came to them at work, in fishing boats, at a wedding, in a storm at sea, when they had questions, on a beach with a campfire, on a road as they were walking, when they were confused, when they had doubts and when they were sulking in defeat.

ELEVATE THE DIGNITY OF WOMEN AND JUDGE NOT

A couple dozen religious lawyers and moralistic men shoved a woman caught in adultery in front of Jesus to stone her and trap him. The rabble of holier-than-thou men, angry and fired up to judge others (the complete opposite of a real good man like Jesus), had rocks at the ready. They were prepared to apply the Jewish law's death penalty for her sin (what about the man's?). Jesus scribbled in the dirt and threw them the question that sent 'em packin'. *"If anyone here has never sinned, feel free to throw the first stone."* He didn't need to speak about the woman's past. He set her free to live forgiven and whole. Judgmentalism and anger don't make a man. They make a hypocrite who hurts people. Men set others free to live better, not lock them up to suffer in punishment and die in shame.

Coaching Strategy—Leave the judging to God. Let's aim to be men who look at the log in our own eyes, challenge angry moralists to do the same, and restore dignity and hope for people with a muddy past. Be a man who doesn't use women, demean women or abuse women. Let's be realists and idealists about sex. It's a beautiful, powerful force meant to bond a man and woman for good. But when people have been abused, deceived, or get desperate for love or survival, the power of sex often damages and traps them.

Be Humble. Leave the judging to God. Look for logs in our own eyes. Dignify women. Rescue the abused. Care for the accused. Elevate and protect sex with exclusivity. Commit to one wife for the rest of your life.

INTENTIONALLY GATHER AND SERVE YOUR FAMILY AND FRIENDS

Jesus built deep friendships. He set up meals, walks, boat rides, silent times in the hills and a special farewell dinner the evening before his arrest (which He and Judas alone knew was coming). Before eating, Jesus, the head of the family and a leader of leaders, shocked his friends with a radical move. He stepped back from his spot at the table, knelt at their feet and took a bowl of water and a towel to wash their grimy feet. Jesus loved and led in the truest and fullest way—He served.

> Real men are marked by authenticity, intimacy, and service to others.

Men who are real and good are authentic and close. They make efforts to gather, serve and bless their family. They make friendship a priority with sacrifice, service and memorable demonstrations of love.

Coaching Strategy—Make dinner and gathering a priority in your family. Be an intentional, committed friend. Plan a meal. Step down to serve. Share a toast. Pray a prayer.

Oh, and expect to get let down, and even betrayed by the 12th guy. Jesus showed us men how to take the risk, get close and never waste energy trying to get even.

Unite the family. Gather your friends. Treat them as special. Make memories. Step down and serve.

Let's summarize the manhood and masculinity of Jesus. He:

- **Was first, foremost, and always—a son.** He lived by receiving His identity, guidance and strength.
- **Fearlessly faced blitzes.** He humbled Himself, faced reality, suffered and died for others to live.
- **Was not upset by scuttled plans or surprising intense challenges.** He was resilient and adaptable. He persevered.
- **Championed underdogs** and comeback stories.
- **Had friends and showed up for them.** He was trusted by his friends because he was present. He cared and He invested.
- **Had a mission to benefit others,** to make lives better, to give life that lasts forever. He didn't work alone.
- **Elevated the dignity of women.** He was counter-cultural. He saw the heart, solved problems and called out hypocrisy and judgmentalism.
- **Had empathy and compassion.** He noticed and met people's physical, emotional, and spiritual needs.
- **Was humble, grateful, optimistic, and resourceful.** He saw no limits to what His Father could do.
- **Was decisive and excellent.** He trained with action and experience, not just with words and instruction.
- **Gathered and served family and friends.** He formed special personalized groups, experiences, and communities.

Guys, we were created and intended to live like this. Adam, Eve, and all of us humans rebelled. We fell. We lost the vision and ability for manhood as intended. But God sent Jesus to restore it with His presence, strength and love.

ASK MYSELF

- "What is preventing me from seeing God accurately and receiving Jesus as my essential way to live as a man?"

MY ACTIONS

- I will acknowledge where I am in my journey and closeness to or distance from God—*I don't see Him as my Father or know Jesus. I'm not sure about or close to Him right now. I believe but am not trusting or experiencing Him. I'm trying to trust but the well is dry.*

- I will hear and respond to Father God's invitation to me: *Come directly as you are. Ask Me to help you reconsider, reframe, and receive My Son, the Real Jesus, so I can forgive you, adopt you as My son and guide you along your journey. Call me Abba, Dad, Father. Ask me to re-Father you and answer your deepest questions. Come to Me as your Abba Father every morning and come to My Word as a son expecting Me to speak to you. Replace lesser things with Jesus as your treasure, model and strength. Let Me transform you and own your life. Let Me show you how to live in the way of Jesus—receiving from Me and teaming up with a few deep friends for my best purposes.*

- Reconsider. Repent. Reconnect. Receive. Revive. Reconcile. Live like Jesus. Live as a beloved son. Live with the strength Jesus brings you.

"No man is trapped except in his own mind."

—**Better Man Ministries**

"The most important thing about you is what you think about when you think about God."

—**JI Packer**

9

ESSENTIAL MANHOOD: HOW TO LIVE IT, THE WAY OF JESUS

A t this point you may be thinking, *I get it, Jeff. You're telling me that the way to be a better man is to be like Jesus.*

Well, yes and no.

Being like Jesus sounds like a great goal, but it's impossible. We just can't do it. Or, more accurately, we can't do it *on our own*.

No more than a kite can fly itself.

Do you remember flying kites when you were a kid? You pulled the kite out of the plastic wrapper, inserted the cross supports, tied a tail on one end, and then attached a string. You were ready to fly.

Out to the nearest open field you'd go. There was no wind, so you started running, first a jog and then a sprint. At first, your kite showed some promise of lift, but then . . . plop. Turns out you just couldn't run fast enough to compensate for the missing breeze.

But then, a few days later you saw tree limbs swaying and you knew what that meant—wind! You grabbed the kite, checked the tail and the string, and headed off for the field again. You only had to run a little this time. The wind rushed underneath the sail of your kite and—up, up, and away! Liftoff. Soon the whole spool of string had unwound, and the kite was at maximum altitude. (Makes me want to fly one right now.)

> God calls me out of a performance-driven culture into a culture of grace, simply being in a relationship with my heavenly Father. BEING precedes DOING.

We grow up and we still approach life like the kid with no breeze. We dream about the kind of man we want to be—in our element, true to our design, soaring. We run and run and run. Sooner or later, we wear out, give up, or crash.

This is the flight pattern for performance-based manhood. But there's a better way.

BEING BEFORE DOING

I get it; we live in a performance-driven culture. We're often judged by our accomplishments. The value others place on us, even the value we give ourselves, is based on our latest win.

The fact is: men are wired to perform. God designed us for adventure, conquering challenges and solving problems—to create and build things, to take care of the people we love, and to improve our world.

So, I'm not knocking the inner drive to work and perform, but there *is* something that needs to come before all this *doing*. And that is—*being*. Instead of running and hoping eventually to have lift, we can catch the wind.

Here's the point: If we don't connect to Father God, we're grounded. No amount of our performance is ever going to match what God can do.

It's not like God gave us a list of goals and instructions on how to accomplish them, then turned us loose to fly or fall. He showed us a model of ideal manhood through His Son, and then offered everything we need to join Him—through a close and lasting relationship.

Being the son of the Father is where our identity is formed—where our lives get lift. *Being* God's son is what allows us to perform as authentic and beneficial men. It's the relationship that brings the wind, the power to live as the man, husband, father, leader, and friend you want to be.

Before moving on to *why* and *how* this approach to manhood works, let me say one thing more about being a son of the Father. In our earthly relationships, we're dependent upon our parents until we want independence and launch out on our own. We're then supposed to support ourselves and live independently.

But things are different when it comes to Father God. With Him, the more we grow, the more we depend on Him. His hold on us gets stronger. We want it to. We *need* it to. Dependence on God makes us wiser. We never outgrow the longing for His love, His presence, His guidance. That's where the power is.

THE *WHY*

I've been at my worst in life when I've not had a clear and compelling purpose—when I'm missing a good *why*. Before you can act meaningfully, you need to have a vision of success.

After finishing a speech, Hellen Keller was asked by a curious college student what could possibly be worse than not being able to see. Miss

Keller promptly replied, "It would be so much worse to have your eyesight but lack vision."

What does that mean for men? Robert Lewis once told me, "If you could open up a man and see his vision—the primal convictions that drive him—you'd see his whole life." Sadly, many men have a vision shaped by a wound from their childhood or the confusion of their culture.

"Without the vision," Robert points out, "a man is aimless at best and dangerous at worst." Without vision, men become aggressive about self-centered things and passive in others-centered things like relationships—particularly with God and a wife. Passive about the most meaningful things, but not about fantasy football, video games, entertainment, and hobbies. Worse than all that, guys without vision may get aggressive about destructive things like chasing money, getting high, or drinking. They get passive about love and loyalty, but not about consuming porn, sex, and women.

The vision for masculinity is Jesus. Manhood comes from a relationship as a son of the Father.

Manhood is commitment, courage, and strength in a cause greater than yourself. That was Jesus, receiving His mission and strength from His Father.

Apart from the proper vision (the why), even respectable efforts at manhood can be easily reduced to *acting* like a Christian. I don't know if you care about or go to church, but for guys that do, can we admit this? Just checking that box is empty and doing it to impress can devolve into shallow moralism. That's not a compelling vision at all. It's a meaningless act that eventually leaves a guy stranded in disappointment. His do-good ways were supposed to deliver a happier life.

But we can't let the fear of failure or of not "getting it right" neutralize us. We shouldn't keep the kite in the drawer. Manhood is not neutral, and it certainly isn't boring. Men were not made to just avoid mistakes.

We were made for mission. We are God's sons, in partnership with Him for epic purposes that transcend ourselves and our lifetimes.

WHAT'S A MAN TO DO?

Robert Lewis looked back to the opening two chapters of Genesis, the start of human history where God chartered man's mission. Robert summarizes these "life-giving responsibilities":

1. Follow God's Word
2. Protect God's women
3. Excel at God's work
4. Better God's world

Just four things. Sounds simple enough, right?

Not exactly. On a daily basis, it means always trusting God, faithfully keeping sexual thoughts and urges under control, working with diligence and excellence, and keeping others' interests ahead of your own. I know I can't live up to it all. I'll fail, get discouraged, and fake it for a while until I just give up.

> My WHY, the reason for my existence, is to live as a son of the perfect Father.

But God has a solution for that too. His solution is—Himself. He's our source for being a man, displayed through His Son's perfect life on earth and His death and resurrection to rescue us. Because of Jesus, the Father is willing to adopt you and me as His fully loved sons. And it's in being God's son that we are empowered to live as real and good men.

Your *why*, the reason for your existence—and for mine—is to live as a son of the perfect Father. If Jesus, the ideal man, lived as a son, then so must we. And because of Him, we can.

How—The Way of Jesus

OK, how do we live it day to day? What's the practical, the *how*? We rely on God to give us these four core patterns of manhood from the life of Jesus:

1. Receive
2. Transform
3. Huddle
4. Lift

1. Receive—Be a Son of the Father

We covered the Receive Principle in Chapter 7. It simply means to take something that is offered to you, with humility, gratitude and enthusiasm.

Since Jesus is our model, how did He *receive* from the Father? How did Jesus know, day in and day out, what the Father wanted Him to do and say? How did He receive wisdom, peace, courage, and power?

Jesus ordered His days around time alone with His Father, and He also talked with Him (prayed) at any given need-filled moment. Jesus said, "No branch can bear fruit by itself; it must remain in the vine. Neither can you bear fruit unless you remain in me." (John 15:4). He was explaining that we cannot have any lasting impact that pleases God and blesses other people without the same connection to the Father.

Jesus likened life to an abundant harvest of fruit which He produces through us when we connect to and receive from Him, like a branch is connected to a vine—

> *⁵I am the Vine, you are the branches. When you're joined with me and I with you, the relation intimate and organic, the harvest is sure to be abundant. Separated, you can't produce a thing. ⁹I've loved*

you the way my Father has loved me. Make yourselves at home in my love. (John 15:5, 9 MSG)

Jesus based his earthly life on connecting to, dialoguing with, and receiving love from His Father. He taught people how to connect to His Father's presence and love in prayer. During his most comprehensive recorded teaching—called the Sermon on the Mount—Jesus gave an invitation to all of us.

[6] *Here's what I want you to do: Find a quiet, secluded place so you won't be tempted to role-play before God. Just be there as simply and honestly as you can manage. The focus will shift from you to God, and you will begin to sense his grace.* [8] *This is your Father you are dealing with, and he knows better than you what you need. With a God like this loving you, you can pray very simply.* (Matthew 6:6, 8 MSG)

If *being* precedes *doing*, then *receiving* is the first phase of *being*. This is where it all begins, taking what God makes available to us so we can live the

> If being precedes doing, then receiving what God makes available to me gives me a life of purpose and transformation.

life of purpose and transformation that He has designed for each of His sons and daughters. Jesus was the epitome of courage and bravery because He drew His confidence from His Father.

2. Transform—Keep being changed by God

Jesus is a transformer. He grew and He helped others grow. He matured under his parents. He sought mentoring and teaching from the rabbis and teachers of Scripture. He submitted to authority. He studied God's Word and took it to heart. He made wisdom central to his behavior. He devoted Himself to friends, mastering humility and making the ultimate sacrifice to defeat death on our behalf. He arose from the dead, appeared in a resurrected state and ascended into heaven. His mission of growing, transforming, and lifting others will prevail and be fulfilled in a perfect and glorious eternal kingdom. His love and justice will prevail; all that is broken will be made new.

Jesus' life was not static, and neither is ours. Unlike the perfect Son of God, we need to change, improve, and *be* transformed. We cannot do this by ourselves, but neither are we passive. God calls us to cooperate through faith, obedience, and trust. When we do, we may be surprised how He will use us to make life better for family, friends, and even strangers.

> Transformation involves my cooperating through faith, obedience, and trust in the changes He is making.

It's worth repeating that when it comes to you and me—we cannot *transform* ourselves; God must do it. He determines the transformation that's needed. He's the power. He gets the credit. This isn't an athlete sculpting his body and honing his agility. This isn't self-help. This is God-help.

And it involves living as a team in deep connection with friends. No one is meant to stay the same. Growing never stops. We're transforming from *As Is* to *To Be*.

3. Huddle—Be committed and real in friendship

Jesus was a team guy. Friendship was His way. He was intentional about friendship. He modeled for us that just as teams need to huddle, friends also need to intentionally and frequently connect so they can help one another. The timeless wisdom of God's message urges us that:

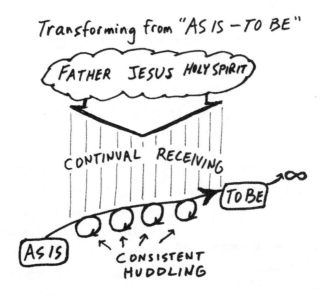

Two friends are stronger together than alone and three are stronger than two. They can help each other sharpen and protect their character. They can coach each other to make better choices with fewer mistakes. They pick each other up in the toughest times, support each other at all times, especially in adversity. God blesses committed friendship, brotherhood, and unity, especially love that sacrifices or dies for a friend. (Based on Ecclesiastes 4; Proverbs 27:17,18; Psalm 133; John 15)

I'll say more about the importance of huddling in a later chapter. For now, I'll summarize it like this: God's instructions to us include the importance of bearing one another's burdens, sharing in one another's joys, grieving together in our losses, and mutually confessing our temptations, weaknesses, mistakes, and sins so we can heal and grow stronger. By disclosing our motives, feelings and plans to

> Huddling is intentionally connecting with friends to grow stronger in the Lord.

one another, we can live in the light and avoid the errors that come from isolation and secrecy. In this level of friendship, we are compelled to meet regularly for enjoyment, support and spiritual growth.

4. Lift—Encourage, support and bring out the best in people and situations

Jesus improved situations and people. He lifted sick, poor, oppressed, and overlooked people to dignity and healing. He lifted others' hopes and sights for a better and eternal future with Him and the Father, so much better than the direction they were going apart from Him. He lifted the confidence and sense of belonging for the "average" guys He brought onto His core team. He lifted them by investing His time, encouragement, training, honesty, affirmation, vision, correction, and forgiveness. He lived the Gideon Principle of giving people their identity, validation and freedom to be their best.

> Lift involves allowing myself to be the means by which God loves and gives hope to others.

Our relationships are a way to channel the love, forgiveness, and generosity God showed us to other people who need His love, hope, and validation. Like Jesus, we are meant to be men who lift others. We're meant to make situations and places better than they were.

Jesus showed us how to live out the essentials of manhood. In essence, His masculinity was the identity He received from His Father and the catalyst for the way He lived each day.

It's meant to be the same for you and me. We gain our identity from God, too. He adopts us as sons when we come to Him through Jesus. Then our story is a turnaround story. We become stewards of what God created. Our work is to follow the ways of Jesus.

What I've described here is not less fun or rewarding than the typical worldly quest for success. On the contrary, the compromises, frustrations, emptiness, and loneliness experienced by so many of the world's most "successful" men prove that God's way is the way of a real and rewarding life.

ASK MYSELF

- "Which is closer to my approach to life?"
  - A. "I own my life and am looking for everything in the here and now on earth."
  - B. "God is my Father and source. Jesus is my leader and satisfaction. I want His Spirit to transform and direct me in the present and aim me for eternity."

MY ACTIONS

- I'm gonna go fly a kite (or paper airplane, if stuck on the couch). And I'll talk with a friend about the kite metaphor that Jesus, His Father, and Spirit are far more dependable than the wind on any particular day. I will discuss how God can fuel my life, instead of trying to fly the kite of my life by aimlessly running around.

Manhood is not self-propelled. It's not self-confident. It's God-confident. It comes from Jesus and our Father—knowing Him as the source of life, love, and mission. It's living in Jesus, abiding as the Father's son who trusts that His way is best and asking for His guidance to follow Him in a dependent relationship.

TRANSFORM

10

FREEDOM IN FORGIVING

A re you better at forgiving or blaming? It's important to figure out because one sets you free and the other poisons you.

Too often the people we expect to support us become villains who drag us down and deeply damage us. Our fight or flight instincts make us blame more than forgive. That makes it really hard to heal—clamping us in the very trap the enemy designs for us.

Escaping the trap becomes way easier when we remember the story of how God forgave us and learn the story behind the person who hurt us.

> Forgiveness sets
> *me* free; blaming
> poisons *me*.

Have you ever found yourself rooting for the villain in a movie after learning his backstory?

The backstory provides context, context allows understanding, and understanding leads to compassion. He or she is more relatable, more vulnerable, more human.

We don't naturally try to understand those who've harmed us, do we? But once you know why your villain acts that way, you might not *root* for him or her—but something will radically change.

EVERYONE HAS A BACKSTORY

Who's the villain in your story? You may have more than one. A parent? A sibling? Someone you grew up with? Is it someone in your life right now?

My friend Josh (not his real name) has a strained relationship with his mother. They got along fine on the surface, but her critical, domineering ways kept Josh from feeling close to her. Mixed in with his feelings of respect for her was resentment.

When Josh opened up to her, she usually brushed his feelings aside. "That's just the way life is," she'd say, or "You shouldn't let that get to you." Josh gave up. He decided to never share anything too close to his heart with her again.

Until his eyes were opened to her backstory.

Josh's mother grew up in a difficult home. The oldest of eight children, her dad was an alcoholic. She never had much of a childhood at all. She assumed grownup duties at a young age and dealt with all the difficulties and stress that alcoholism added to daily life.

Once Josh knew her backstory, his compassion for her grew. Even though she didn't change, Josh could understand, and even admire, how she lived through the hardship. Then, he wondered about his grandfather's backstory—because he had one too.

REMEMBER YOUR VILLAIN HAS A NAME

Here's a tool to help you start understanding your villains. Call them by their first name, even if it's your mom or dad.

Why?

Because our names humanize us. They pull our villains off the pedestal of unrealistic expectations and remind us that they were once children. They still have their own wounds, insecurities and fears.

Hopefully, you find yourself thinking of them not as villains, but as people.

That person who hurt you is a person with a name and backstory. A person who has, more than likely, been hurt themselves.

Does that excuse their behavior? Absolutely not. But it will help *you* move forward without dragging along the weight of bitterness.

> Hurt people hurt others. I must learn the backstory of the one who has hurt me.

STEVE LARGENT'S STORY

When Steve Largent and I became friends, he was a Pro Bowl Wide Receiver for the Seattle Seahawks with an intense competitive edge and a legendary work ethic. Like all of us, he had a backstory.

Steve's dad left his family when he was only six years old. After that, he saw his dad just once before graduating high school—and only because they both attended a court hearing. His dad wanted to know what benefits Steve and his siblings were getting so he wouldn't have to pay child support. As Steve recalls, "Definitely not a positive or healing meeting with my missing dad."

Steve filled that father-void with work and football. You could say he was in the 'Struggle' season of his life. His drive for success made everyone on his teams better. He was the ultimate teammate, but he'd need the help of the teammates closest to him.

First, his wife Terry.

When Steve's father resurfaced after decades away, it was only to ask for game tickets. "I was going to blow him off," Steve admits. But Terry convinced him to try to establish some kind of relationship.

"I was willing to meet him after the game. I met his wife and kids. There was nothing more than that, no genuine interest by either of us. He'd call me when we had games in cities near Philly. I'd buy him a couple tickets and a room near our hotel. Then he started asking for 4 . . . 6 . . . 8 tickets. I did it. But it grated on me."

When Steve turned 25, he learned that his dad had also grown up in a blended family and shared other similarities. His dad was a high school football hero in a small city. Then he got a scholarship to Oklahoma State. He was a rough and tough guy. He married Steve's mom when he was just twenty-one and she was twenty.

Steve's dad's backstory and his own backstory had similarities, but their following stories diverged. His dad wasn't exposed to caring people like Steve was. And through these friendships, Steve was introduced to a relationship with God. He received Jesus before heading off to college and that relationship became the center of his life.

As Steve matured, he began to understand his dad's story. "Dad was an insecure guy, despite what he showed on the surface as a Marine sergeant."

Steve saw that his dad never had the opportunity that Steve did to have a handful of close and loyal friends who walked with God. "He was probably pretty isolated. He married and divorced three times, with kids in each marriage. He was hurting. He basically had to figure out life, manhood, marriage and family on his own."

He understood his father's backstory but still couldn't let go.

And when Steve retired from football, even those brief contacts stopped. "I completely closed myself off emotionally to my dad."

How would you have felt if your dad came back for tickets, not reconciliation? For a transaction, not a relationship? Can you feel the heavy wrench in your gut? Do you feel the hole inside a man who still has the wounded heart of a little boy?

Think about the frustration, the bitterness, the hard shell that formed. Imagine waiting decades for a gesture, an acknowledgment, an apology—and not getting it. Steve was trapped in these emotions.

FORGIVE THOSE WHO HURT YOU

One of the manliest things you will ever do requires no workouts, tools, or brute force. It's answering the call to forgive someone who wronged you.

Today, Steve is free. But it took help from more teammates to forgive his dad.

Next was Marty Sherman. It was an intentional friendship Steve made as part of a weekly huddle. Marty, Steve and four other committed peers became close friends. "Being there was

> True manliness forgives those who have wronged me. Forgiveness sets me free.

sacrosanct. Canceling wasn't an option. Not showing wasn't allowed. We were all committed."

It was a place for total openness and honesty *because* each man learned the others' backstories. Steve remembered, "I told the guys my story, about my dad leaving us when I was six—that I'd only seen him a couple of times—that I didn't really know him. One week, I told Marty that my dad was moving back to Tulsa, our hometown."

Marty called him the day after their weekly huddle. He said, "Steve, I have an impression that you need to reach out to rebuild something with your dad. I think this is an opportunity for you to get a burden off your back."

He explained, "You need to forgive your father—not to set him free, but to set yourself free. It's about doing the right thing. That's what the Lord calls you to do. If you're genuine and sincere, it'll set you free."

Motivated by his friend's wisdom, Steve called his dad and set up breakfast. He took another bit of Marty's advice: to start the awkward meeting off by *making* an apology to his dad.

Can you imagine the humility it takes to *apologize* to someone who has wronged you?

Steve spoke first, "I want to ask you to forgive me for not calling you when I could have or seeking you out over the years." His dad started crying. He admitted to Steve that he felt bad that they had not had a better relationship.

There was no grand change. His dad didn't become a different man and the relationship never transformed into the ideal one Steve might have dreamed about. Even just three miles away in Tulsa, he never pursued a relationship with Steve.

"I didn't have expectations that he'd do anything differently," Steve recalled. "But I had set myself free from the bitterness and the wound that festered."

It took God's forgiveness, listening to his wife, listening to Marty, and entrusting himself to a few deep friends to convince Steve to reach out to his dad again. And it took courage for him to apologize for the relatively small role he'd played in the rift, and then to forgive his dad.

As Steve's friend, and as a man, I'm impressed. And convicted. Am I holding any resentment? What could unforgiveness be costing me?

FORGIVING REQUIRES STRENGTH

Author Andrée Seu Peterson writes, "Forgiving is the hardest thing you will ever do. That's why most people don't do it. I asked a few people if they'd ever forgiven anyone, and what it felt like. They gave me answers so pious I knew they'd never done it."

Why is it so hard? Because it feels wrong. We were hurt. Often it was intentional, not by accident—and we're supposed to just let them get away with it?

Know this: There is nothing weak about forgiving. It's not caving in. It takes courage and great strength. You don't walk *away* from the hurt. You walk *through* it. You feel the pain, reject every inclination to get even and come back to your offender with something undeserved—love and grace.

> Forgiveness is not a sign of weakness, but of strength. It's walking through the pain and offering undeserved love and grace to the offender.

Forgiving is not coping. Coping retains the divide. Forgiving resolves it. It ends the constant replaying of the injury, the hurt, the anger and bitterness. You'll choose to stop being a victim. You quit wanting them to be punished. You choose to regain your power and move on.

As Steve would tell you, the great gain is worth the cost. Resentment has residual effects, undermining our emotional and spiritual health. Steve says that forgiving his dad freed him from the pain he carried for years and allowed him to break through to a new level of maturity in life and relationships. He was no longer a victim. His character grew. His family and children benefitted. He reached the *Significance* season of life—he set an example for me and the rest of us.

You might feel skeptical of this message. It might make you mad. You may think this kind of forgiveness is weak, foolish or just impossible. You may be a guy who had trauma in his life—a dad who abandoned or belittled you. A warped man who sexually abused you as a child. An ex-wife who hired full-combat lawyers to emasculate and impoverish you—maybe even building a legal chasm between you and your child. I am sorry. I can't fix any of that. But there is a best way forward.

JESUS SHOWED US HOW TO FORGIVE

The strongest man in the world showed us the answer. He forgave. And He gave us the power to forgive. The power to set ourselves free from the bitterness, resentment, and anger. The power to set ourselves free from the past. Hanging on a cross, near his last breaths, Jesus gasped, "Father, forgive them—for they don't know what they are doing."

The people who offend and hurt us are imperfect, like us. They have a backstory. They need forgiveness, just like we do, for all we have done. The only man who ever lived perfectly, Jesus, bought that forgiveness when He chose to die for us, and then rose from the dead. He forgave us more than we will ever have to forgive others.

People who have been greatly forgiven forgive others. Have you fully received the greatest forgiveness from God? That is the key and the catalyst to you forgiving others.

The best of manhood is being like Jesus. He paid the ultimate price to forgive. His mission was to reconcile, and He succeeded. He gave us the same mission. (Forgiving is crucial to reconciling but so is something else that Jesus never had to do—apologize. We'll get to that, too.)

Are you ready to be free? Forgive and you'll become a peacemaker. Like Steve, you can stop feeling like a victim and gain the power to move forward. You can turn your relationships with your parents or your past around. You can turn your marriage around. You can move closer to your children or your team—and make a better future possible.

Forgiving is huge. It's a man thing. It's a Jesus thing. Like Steve, like Josh, you can forgive with His help and move forward in a much better way.

ASK MYSELF

- "What grade do I give myself in forgiving? Would Jesus agree?"
- "Do I expect and handle blitzes Jesus' way? Do I turn to my Father? Keep a team-mindset? Envision the long-term? Be humble and willing to change? Focus on blessing others?"

MY ACTIONS

- By God's grace, I won't fall for the *Fundamental Attribution Error** which blames other people's failures on their character and excuses my own failures as due to outside circumstances.
- I will ask God, "Show me what I don't know and need to understand about their backstory. What should I do and how?" Rule of thumb: ask God and you'll get better instruction than from any book.
- Ideas: I will write down why I'm bitter and haven't forgiven that person or persons. I will compare God's forgiveness to my lack of forgiveness. I will write "canceled" over what I have not forgiven. I will demonstrate my forgiveness as personally as possible—perhaps starting with an apology.

Pride poisons an offense with resentment and bitterness. Unforgiveness poisons our soul. Humility heals with a forgiveness that sets us and others free.

---

* The Fundamental Attribution Error is the tendency to overemphasize personal characteristics and ignore situational factors in judging others' behavior. Because of it, we tend to believe others do bad things because they are bad people. We're inclined to ignore situational factors that might have played a role. Source: https://ethicsunwrapped.utexas.edu/glossary/fundamental-attribution-error

11

STRONG IS HUMBLE

D o you want to be strong? Do you want to live with courage? Do you want to overcome obstacles, recover from setbacks and succeed?

We all do.

We go along enjoying success and puffing out our chests. Then one day, we're beaten at arm-wrestling or lose at bowling (of all things). We get older and we're passed over for a job, beaten out by the competition. Suddenly, we feel like a weakling. We beat ourselves up.

Brother, please don't assess your strength as a man by how you compare to or compete with other men (good news if our Instagram or arm-wrestling form is flimsy). What's more, that kind of strength is both elusive and, at the end of the day, false.

Here's more good news. There is a true way to measure strength.

Want to know the essence of real and good strength? It benefits others—dependably and courageously. Jesus already modeled it for us. He used his strength for others, not for Himself.

He was God on earth. Imagine the feats of physical strength he could have performed to prove it. Instead, he knelt down before a woman who was caught in adultery. His courage protected her from the self-righteous mob, his true compassionate strength presenting a stark contrast to the violent bravado of the crowd.

> The essence of true strength is how it benefits others.

Did He celebrate himself as His disciples' epic leader on their last night together? Not even close. He served them by washing their grimy feet. Then He prepared them for what was to come—His betrayal by Judas and Peter's denials.

Courageous, compassionate, dependable and, above all, focused on others. *That* is the essence of true strength.

But how can we rise to His example?

This strength comes from our roots before it ever shows up in our actions. *Being* comes before *doing*. Therefore, we must receive an identity—one that has the power to be truly strong because it comes from our Father in Heaven. That power is not the money, muscles, or influence of worldly identities.

It's Jesus Himself. To draw from His power, we must lower ourselves like a thirsty man to a well. When we admit that we need Him, God uses our weaknesses, strengths, and abilities—not for our own ends, but for others.

JORDAN

A couple years ago, I went with seven guys on a retreat to the Bitterroot River in Montana, hoping to create a friendship experience where we could orient our lives to become better men. We wanted to be men who make life better for our wives and children, men who improve life for those we know and care about. We talked for hours, sharing stories both hilarious and painful. There was a power we gained by disclosing things that aren't talked about often.

There, we also met Jordan, a man who embodied the kind of strength I'm talking about. The six-foot, slender, dark-haired, and impressively calm local was our fly-fishing guide for the weekend.

He handled everything—I mean, everything. We didn't drive or row. We never even got wet. Our lunch showed up at the perfect time. Our boat found its way to the best spots. He quickly freed any snagged lines. And he never made us feel dumb, needy or weak.

Turns out, there was a reason why he was so good at serving others. As I asked him questions, I discovered he had volunteered for the Army after 9/11. He served in the Special Forces—four tours to the Middle East and three to Southeast Asia.

After 11 years, Jordan left the military. He wanted the chance to live a normal life with his wife and children after so much time on the battle-field. He lost many friends and comrades in those deployments and three more to alcohol-related deaths and suicide after they came home.

Jordan told me he finds his life on the river in Montana therapeutic. My hunch? His dedication to serving others has brought the greatest heal-ing. When he's guiding, he's fully dedicated to the needs of his guests.

As we drove back to camp in his pickup, I asked Jordan how he faced the risk of death during his deployments. He explained that he had to count himself as dead before he went on a mission—two days of constant danger and no sleep. Accepting his possible death freed his mind to be fully aware, focused on doing everything to protect his squad and accomplish the mission. Once, under heavy fire, his buddy behind him was hit. Jordan dragged him 200 meters through a drainage ditch to medics.

Jordan lives, and was willing to die, for others. Many of us *want* to be just like him, but we aren't surrounded by a group of men bringing out the best in each other and living for a cause greater than ourselves.

Imagine how strong you would be if you counted yourself dead like Jordan did.

Dead to achieving vain goals—like getting more money, success, fame, or significance. Dead to the comfort and illusions of control ingrained in you by our culture. What if you counted yourself dead to winning arguments and getting your way?

> True manly strength begins with counting yourself dead!

Count yourself dead and see how much easier it is to serve. Could you deliver your wife or family from your selfishness, defensiveness and pride? Would you have more empathy? Will it give you the *power* to lead in the radical way that Jesus did? Can you humble yourself and lift others instead?

Through Christ, I can. And so can you. Will I? Will you?

PRIDE-HUMILITY PARADOX

If you look at well-known cases of pride, there's a clear connection between their attitudes, actions and consequences. (I don't mean to shame these people—and certainly don't mean to say that I could have handled the talent, popularity, or success any better.)

Why was President Clinton willing to risk political standing with his adolescent behavior?

Why did Tiger Woods inflict so much damage on his family, reputation and career?

What drove Bernie Madoff to steal and deceive in ways that were sure to be discovered?

What caused the downfall of gifted Christian leaders like Mark Driscoll and Ravi Zacharias?

Since we *are* naming names, I might as well ask: What drives *me* to defend myself and criticize others? What makes me so slow to apologize? (My failings might not be as public as theirs, but they're just as real).

Lust and greed certainly played a part. But I think it's something deeper.

What made them think their actions were okay? What makes us think our selfishness is?

Everyone thinks, deep down, *I am special.* And special people get a pass, we think, even if it's for behavior we find despicable in others. Pride traps us in this self-centered bubble of entitlement. Maybe we think our position or personality makes us immune to the consequences of our actions.

This person, or sometimes a group of people, believes themselves superior to others, or immune to consequences. They embrace an *Us versus Them* mentality that leads to superiority, entitlement, and compromise. It can fuel prejudice or worse.

> Pride can easily trap me in a self-centered bubble of entitlement, making me unaware of the consequences of my actions.

Pride blinds. Pride divides. Pride damages. Pride destroys.

Pride is a killer.

It makes me think of my painful midseason loss as a Seattle Seahawk in a *Sunday Night Football* game.

We were up in the 4th quarter. As a team, we were feeling good about ourselves. We were so comfortable with our lead, we credited ourselves with a win before the game was over.

Pride set us up—and brought us down.

I remember thinking, *"This game has gone pretty well! It'll be good to have a win."* The coaches must have thought the same. The game plan shifted to running out the clock. The defense started playing prevent defense (the only thing it *prevented* was a win!). On offense, the play-calling went cautious, and we played flat. Meanwhile, the Raiders got hot and started scoring. I threw a pass that was caught by a friend. Problem—he was on the wrong team. We lost in sudden death, and I was cut two days later.

Talk about humbling.

So, what's the cure?

GRAB YOUR OXYGEN MASK!

I'll never forget what my friend Don Wallis told me about how, as a Naval fighter pilot, he was trained to deal with the sudden loss of oxygen.

When a pilot loses oxygen, it's so subtle and gradual that the individual typically doesn't even know it before losing consciousness. To prepare trainees for the phenomenon, the Navy seats two pilots across from each other in a sealed chamber with an oxygen tank and mask next to each. The pair play rock-paper-scissors while instructors watch through a window and slowly reduce the oxygen.

As soon as one begins to feel the effects, he or she can simply put on the mask and recover. But they usually don't.

Don explained how the competitive spirit takes over—neither pilot wants to be the first to *need* oxygen. More importantly, the oxygen depletion deceives their brains. They get spastic, then lethargic. Their lack of oxygen keeps them from realizing that they *need* oxygen. Someone from outside the chamber has to tell them what to do.

It's the same with pride. We hardly know it's taking over, causing us to lose awareness of those around us and the consequences of our actions.

Do you have a man outside the chamber? The guy who has permission to wake you up and tell you the uncomfortable truth when you need it most?

Even after the training, Don was "a bit cocky" by his own admission and didn't always have his oxygen mask strapped into position because it was uncomfortable to wear. Then one day, he and his training officer were flying in separate planes, preparing for dogfighting training. To mark the start of the dogfight, the officer radioed, "Turn in."

But Don didn't turn in.

The training officer barked again, "Turn in!"

Again, Don did not.

At this point, the officer knew something was wrong. He quickly guessed Don was losing oxygen and wasn't understanding his commands. With seconds to act, he amped up the volume and said, "Don! Grab your oxygen mask! Now! Put it on!"

Don groggily responded and quickly regained full consciousness. Fifteen seconds more and he would have nosedived into the ocean.

> Pride will bring you down if you don't have someone to call you out of your stupor.

That is how quickly pride sinks us if we don't have someone to call us out of our stupor.

THE POWER OF HUMBLE

So, we've seen the weakness and insecurity of pride. On the other side of the paradox is the surprising power of humility.

In his classic book, *Good to Great,* business guru Jim Collins identified the unique type of leadership that transformed good companies into great ones. On a scale of 1 to 5, Level 5 leaders keep their team focused with an indomitable will and have a personal humility that catalyzes excellent team culture and collaboration.

Southwest Airlines surpassed the competition, powered by the servant leadership of CEO Herb Kelleher. His passion was for people. Over half a century, he honored the value, interests, and potential of his entire team—and led Southwest to 46 consecutive years of profitability. Kelleher summed it up in one brilliant sentence: "I'd rather have a company bound by love than a company bound by fear."

Being humble and creating an excellent company is a huge feat. So is *staying* humble.

In 2014, Steve Kerr reshaped the Golden State Warriors by giving them a simple team goal: pass the ball 300 times per game. On a team of superstars—in a league of superstars—his goal was revolutionary. It promoted humility. Giving up their own chance to score, the teammates served each other and set each other up for success for the good of the team.

How often have we heard a team's season attributed to the humility of the coaches and players? *What a humble bunch. Everyone works to help others succeed. These guys love each other . . .*

Unfortunately, pride usually sneaks in before the next preseason begins. After the rings, the contract negotiations and the endorsement deals, players want the credit, the glory and the money. It's hard to turn away from these individualistic goals and focus on the team.

As I write this, the Warriors have gone 467-236 under Kerr, reaching the NBA Finals six times and winning four championships. Kerr's brilliant rule, as well as his own servant leadership, has kept them humble—and kept them winning.

THE POWER AND THE PARADOX

Jesus said a lot of countercultural things. Among the most shocking? "Blessed are the meek, for they shall inherit the earth" (Matthew 5:5 ESV). Clearly, meekness is not the weakness we think it is. Meekness is the strength to submit to God and sometimes to others. Meekness is born out of humility.

> **Biblical humility and meekness are evidence of strength, not weakness.**

The Bible also says, "It is better to be of a lowly spirit with the poor than to divide the spoil with the proud" (Proverbs 16:19 ESV). That was written by King Solomon—an extremely powerful man recognized as the wisest of his time.

The paradox of pride and humility is this: what culture pushes as strength is miserably weak and what it scorns as weakness is truly strong. Pride, we're told, is strength. It's how we win. Humility, on the other hand, is weak. Humility is for losers.

But I call BS! We've already seen how the opposite is true when it comes to real life—for companies, for teams, for military squads.

It's just as obvious in everyday life.

Who do you enjoy hanging out with more? Arrogant guys who make everything all about them? Or humble guys who show you they care about you?

We've already established that we're okay with our own pride, but we can't stand arrogance in others, can we?

Want to see it even more clearly? Think about it as a dad. Do you want your daughter to marry the guy that brags about everything he does or the guy who puts his head down and gets his work done? The guy who's his own biggest fan or the guy who's quick with a compliment and celebrates your daughter's wins even more than his own? The guy who constantly spends money on himself or the guy who is content and generous? The guy who bristles at advice from your daughter or the guy who asks questions and listens to her? The guy who won't ask for help or apologize or the guy who asks for help and doesn't hesitate to apologize when he's made a mistake?

The choice is obvious. But what about your wife? Which guy do you want for *her?* Which guy will bring more health, harmony, and happiness to *your* home?

And let's not forget—The strongest, most courageous, most influential and successful leader in history, the man who overcame the most injustice, the man who has rescued, saved, and transformed innumerable people (and continues to do so), the man who lived without sinning, the man who loved perfectly—the only One who voluntarily died for others' punishment and then came alive again, is the humblest man ever. Jesus, who by His own admission was "gentle and lowly in heart" (Matthew 11:29 ESV), is humility personified.

With Christ as our model, we see that humility comes through self-forgetfulness—not an unhealthy neglect but putting God first and others second. As many have said, *I am third*—like Jordan counting himself dead.

> "Humility is not thinking less of yourself; it's thinking of yourself less."
> (C.S. Lewis)

When we remember God's view of us, we don't need to be self-centered, self-concerned or even self-conscious. We don't stress about what's best for us or what people think of us or do to us. We'll be less likely to offend and less offendable ourselves.

Author Bart Hansen points out that truly humble people "have so little to lose or gain from the approval of others." C.S. Lewis succinctly adds, "Humility is not thinking less of yourself; it's thinking of yourself less."

Let's live on the right side of the paradox, where humility is strength and self-promotion is a thing of the past.

ASK MYSELF

- "How is my pride impacting relationships? On a 1 to 10 scale from terrible pride to pure humility, how is my pride impacting my view of myself? my behavior and vices? my connection to God? friends? coworkers? my wife or girlfriend? kids?"

MY ACTIONS

- Today and tomorrow, I will focus my interest on others by asking questions about them and their life. I'll aim not to talk about myself at all. I will shut up, listen and ask another question. (Perhaps I'll try this for a whole week, then I can go back to being self-absorbed—or not. HA.)

"Humility is the foundation of all the other virtues hence, in the soul in which this virtue does not exist there cannot be any other virtue except in mere appearance."

—Saint Augustine

12

INSECURITY—WHAT ARE THEY THINKING ABOUT ME?

D
o you wonder what other people think of you? It's a pretty common affliction—and a total waste of energy.

As for me, I'm well acquainted with the feelings of insecurity. From the shame I felt over losing a wrestling match in the 5th grade (see chapter 3), to oversized fear and hesitance around girls I liked, to comparing myself to my dad when I was on the bench as a third-string Dartmouth quarterback, hiding my feelings was a way of life for many years.

IF ONLY

Some of us never seem to get out of insecurity's grip. Everything we consider to be "wrong" about us has to be hidden. We can't show weakness. So, insecurity mixes with pride and we are trapped.

I lost my friend Grant Feasel at age 52. His wife Cyndi and his kids Sean, Spencer, and Sarah lost far more. Their lives were shattered.

Grant was a center and long-snapper in the NFL for ten seasons. He was hard working, responsible, and family oriented. He was a great roommate and friend. He went on to be successful in medical sales after retiring from the NFL.

Grant was a good man. He had Christian faith, but his self-awareness was damaged, making it hard for him to see beyond the pain in his joints and the growing confusion in his brain. He couldn't bring himself to admit these growing weaknesses, and that created gaps in his friendships and in his family relationships.

This may sound far-fetched, but I think Grant's troubles began to surface twenty years earlier. I was the Seahawks' holder for field goals. Grant would always agree to stay after practice for extra snaps, but when I asked him to fire some high, low, inside, and wide snaps to help me practice for bad snaps, he refused. "They're always watching, from the roof or cameras, Jeff. I can't show them any bad snaps."

Grant knew the NFL was a performance-driven environment. Getting benched or cut was often on players' minds. (On the inside, "NFL" also stood for *Not For Long*.) But Grant may have had a case of hyper-insecurity and excessive self-consciousness. Too much fear.

Grant wasn't a bragger, but he still had a pride problem—the kind of pride that doesn't want to need help, show weakness, or be vulnerable. He feared dropping his guard, and this very thing contributed to his decline and death.

Grant likely didn't realize that his brain was hitting mid-stage chronic traumatic encephalopathy (CTE). Though he'd never been a drinker, when ibuprofen and other medicines weren't enough, he self-medicated with a mix of Diet Sprite, ice, and vodka. Eventually, his Sprite-vodka mix in a super-sized plastic cup was always at hand.

His brother Greg, and others, tried to help Grant. A few stints at rehab didn't stick and Grant quit trying. Greg pleaded in an email for Grant to face reality and get help:

It's my opinion that you are on the verge of irreversible damage in regard to your family, your job, your name, and heaven forbid, your life. Your family loves you and supports you, but not the lies or the drinking. Today, I'm offering my love, my support, and my resources. If you continue to listen to the Vodka, you will lose your kids, your car, your job, your house, and it will be too late to reach out for help.

Please take this in the way it's intended. One brother to another with love and respect.

Grant "Fighting Feasel" was never afraid of defensive powerhouses across the line of scrimmage, but he had a fear of failure on the inside. A fear of being weak. A fear of admitting his flaws. A fear of asking for help that left him alone to drink until his liver failed and his family and friends lost him.

I write this with love for Grant, deep sorrow for his family, and hope that the rest of us can learn from his story. Fighting through insecurity and the fear of appearing flawed is crucial to receiving God's strength to overcome.

What I've learned about myself is that I don't mind feeling underestimated as an underdog or late bloomer, but I absolutely hate feeling like I got my chance and I failed. So, I tend to move the focus to the future and double down on optimism.

In my last season with the Seahawks, we lost a crucial division game, our second in a row. I had not played well. In the postgame interviews, I put on my optimistic face and spoke mostly about how we'd work harder and pick ourselves up and play better next week. I didn't talk about my own performance or responsibility as the quarterback.

Players and coaches pay attention to interviews, so a couple of days later our free safety, Eugene Robinson, pulled me aside and told me that a number of defensive coaches and players were not happy with me. They felt that, by not taking responsibility for our loss, I wasn't being a stand-up guy. They were questioning my character as a teammate and leader. I'd never felt pain in my gut like that.

Eugene was in my inner circle of deep friends—brothers—on the team. I'm so thankful that he cared enough to give me hard truth that I couldn't see. Afterwards, I went to several coaches and players to own up to my responsibility and apologize for downplaying my shortcomings as a leader and QB.

THE POWER OF HONESTY

Is honesty worth the risk? I'm talking about the kind of honesty where I own up to and admit the truth about myself. All of it, not just the good stuff.

In the last chapter, we talked about the paradox that pride makes us weak, and humility makes us strong. Let's dig into another one: The fear of looking like a failure makes us fail.

No surprise, but once again I have to offer myself as an example.

> **The fear of looking like a failure makes us fail.**

I was heading home from a mountain bike ride one hot, humid morning when an idea hit me: *I can grab a quick dip in the neighborhood pool. Yeah. That's exactly what I need.*

Never mind that the pool was closed. And never mind that I had sneaked in once before when it was closed, and Stacy had asked me never to do it again. In fact, she had repeated the request that very morning as I was leaving for my ride.

It's almost like she knew I'd be tempted. Not almost. She knows me!

But the heat, humidity, and sweat outdueled my sense of rightness and her wise advice. As I approached the pool, I peeked around the corner to make sure no one was around. Seeing that I was in the clear, I quickly pulled myself over the six-foot fence and quietly slid into the deep end, making sure to keep my head just above the water line. I enjoyed a cool soak for a couple of minutes and then escaped back over the fence.

But just as I cleared it, an alarm went off. With our house being only a few hundred yards away, I was hoping Stacy wouldn't hear the alarm, put two and two together, and know that her headstrong husband had done exactly what she asked him not to.

I quickly calculated the odds of being able to clear the area before the security guard showed up. I liked my chances, so quickly grabbed my bike behind the nearby bushes and made my way home without getting caught as the dripping-wet mountain biker.

I had risked having our neighborhood pool privileges canceled. That would have been bad news to Stacy and heartbreak to our grandkids. Just the thought of the humiliation I'd nearly brought upon myself shamed me. I hate feeling like a failure in Stacy's eyes. I let the shame decide my strategy. Stay quiet and hope there wasn't any video surveillance to track me down. I wasn't gonna volunteer the story to her anytime soon. Maybe never.

I sat on that secret for over a year.

Now, since I'm writing about honesty and vulnerability, I need to admit that my sneaky pool caper wasn't the first time I had muted Stacy's advice. Years earlier, when I had taken my then 12-year-old son and one of his friends night-skiing, Stacy had asked me not to leave them alone for any reason. But Jeff did what Jeff does, and I left them so I could ski some quick powder on a short steep section no one skied (since it was unlit!). It did not go well. I didn't see a 3-foot drop and face planted in an ice-packed cat track. By the time I made it back to the lift line to meet up with my son and buddy, I was a woozy mess with a bloody face and concussion.

That time, hiding had not been an option.

So, you can see why I was in no hurry to let Stacy know that I was the one who had set off the alarm at the neighborhood pool. (And you can also see why she felt the need to issue cautions to me from time to time.) A live-in-the-moment guy like me needs a think-it-through woman like her. And vice-versa.

Okay, so no real harm done this time, right? No bloody nose. No concussion. And I had gotten away with it. Except, I didn't get away with it. Not really. Here's why: When I keep a secret, I'm not being honest. I'm not relating to Stacy as the complete and actual me. I'm holding something back. I'm not being real. Not being honest with myself is not facing reality. I'm eroding my integrity—and more.

> **When there's a secret between us, there's a gap between us.**

God's idea for marriage is for two to be one—full connection and unity. But even the smallest deception or secret can begin moving the two apart. Where there could be intimacy, there's a gap. And if that gap is not soon closed, mistrust and suspicion begin to eat away at the core of the relationship.

Would I have been embarrassed if I'd admitted to Stacy what I'd done? *Yes.*

Would my kids have lost a bit of respect for me? *Maybe, but only for a moment. Mostly they would've laughed.* (Which is what they did when I finally told them.)

Would I have had to own up to being selfish and quite dumb? *For sure.*

Would dealing with all of that have actually helped my character? *No doubt.*

Would honesty have restored Stacy's trust and respect in me a lot sooner? *Absolutely.*

And would humility and honesty have helped me feel more secure in God's love and acceptance? *Oh, yeah. Remember, His love and acceptance is unconditional!*

So why did I want to hide a quick dip in the neighborhood pool and a rogue solo ski run over a simple admission of momentary foolishness?

Fear. Fear of looking like a failure. Fear of disappointing. Fear of looking stupid.

And so, I repeat: The fear of looking like a failure makes us fail.

COMEBACK STORIES

Jesus urged His followers to be honest, no matter how far they'd drifted, no matter how hard they'd fallen. He celebrated comebacks. He gravitated toward those who'd crashed and was tough on those who faked how good they were. He loved rescues.

Jesus was speaking to you and me, not just the Pharisees, when He told the story about an amazing father, a prodigal son, and an older jealous brother. The younger son pried the inheritance from his dad and took off to hang out in the red-light district. Meanwhile, his older brother stayed home and followed the rules. But he had his own problems: a superiority complex, an ego given to comparing and condemning, and, ironically, his own sense of entitlement. In their own way, each of these brothers had distanced themselves from the goodness and generosity of their father. One did it from a far country, the other while living under the same roof.

Even though it took some rough days to get there, the younger son came clean, told the truth, and chose to be honest with his dad. He woke up and faced reality. He came home, got honest, and confessed it all. He chose humility.

Things went dramatically better than he could imagine. His dad blew him away with affection, forgiveness, and kindness. He gave him a new robe, new sandals, a gold ring, and a killer party, complete with prime veal.

But the older brother refused to join the celebration. Doing so would have meant owning up to the junk that was in his own heart—arrogance, judgment and bitter resentment. Sadly, at the point where the story cuts off, he's missing out—not just on the party, but also on a real and loving relationship with his dad and his brother. He chose pride.

> Being real makes for a life without secrets, gaps, or isolation.

Jesus' story is showing us what kind of father His Father really is. He's also telling us how to approach Him. Be humble. Be honest. Be real. Don't even try to hide your fears and flaws from Him.

This way of relating to the Father is also the path to the best connection of unity in friendship, family, and even romance. It brings closeness, trust and excellence. Being real makes for a life without secrets, gaps, or isolation.

WHAT DAVID SAID

David Robbins is a gifted leader. He has served in international and cross-cultural ministry, launched an entrepreneurial Christian mission in New York City, and now serves as president and CEO of FamilyLife, where I used to work.

David and I had a conversation about the nuances of "being real." I wanted to hear his take on it because I'd heard enough of his story to know there had been a time when he had to learn to become transparent and vulnerable. He and I have both worked in highly visible roles and we both admit to searching for significance through being "up front" leaders. I knew that David had turned the corner from that misguided search. I wanted to learn what he'd done and how it worked.

So, I asked, "How did you turn from trying to be impressive to simply being *real*?"

David told me about a season of life when he had been "shoved to the sidelines of obscurity." Being a fellow extrovert, I felt a sting in my gut when I heard the word *obscurity*. That is not a happy place for outgoing guys who love to lead like David and me.

"Be ready to learn when God pulls you into places of obscurity or forces you to the sidelines," David said.

Ready to learn—that's sound advice. Anytime God moves us out of our comfort zone, away from our place of cozy familiarity, He's about to teach us something new. Something important.

David went on to describe two seasons of obscurity. One was a stint overseas when he just could not seem to learn the language, and the other occurred when he and his wife faced the birth of a special needs baby followed by a next pregnancy that was a crisis pregnancy. The frustrations and fears of these times seemed to kick both temptations and doubts into overdrive. David began to seriously question whether he belonged in ministry at all.

Eventually David took a couple of deliberate steps toward finding help. The first was to search what the Bible has to say. He remembered the story of Hosea and his habitually unfaithful wife. As David read that story again and again, and meditated on its meaning, he began to see God's character in the way Hosea dealt with marital betrayal. God was like this radically forgiving husband who kept pursuing, caring for, and loving his wife—no matter what she had done to sink their relationship.

"I had to wrestle with the reality that God's love for me was all grace and never earned," David explained. "I was learning to value absolute dependence on God. I had to wrestle with real humility, or what the Bible calls 'boasting in my weakness.'"

His next step was bold, but crucial. "I risked telling a few key men everything that was tempting me. One guy burned me. But, the other three friends took me to deep places of connection with God and with them. As a result, I made a commitment to myself that within six months of moving to any new place to live or work, I would choose someone there to tell my whole story to, along with any struggles or temptations that I faced."

> Transparency is being honest about our past experiences and failures. Vulnerability is being honest about the struggle and risk we're facing right now; while we're still in the middle of it.

God had pulled down David's facade of having it all together and helped him to see that, in his words, "real confidence comes from God, not ourselves."

So, being shoved to the sidelines of obscurity actually served him in a vital way. He met God there.

Deep down, men, we want to be known and accepted for who we actually are. We want to open up, but we need help. This book is about hope and progress for men. It's about helping us become more honest and authentic, about becoming more helpful and loving to others. There's only one way we can get there. Only one way we can change. Only one way we can recover from the past and make ourselves and the future better.

That way revolves around honesty. We need to stop fearing what others think of us. Stop chasing performance and prosperity, or image, so we can get honest in relationships. Stop comparing ourselves to others. Stop making excuses or pretending we're fine.

Honesty brings a stop to the madness of insecurity.

ASK MYSELF

- "With what persons or audience am I afraid to be honest about my struggles, weaknesses and failures?"

MY ACTIONS

- If I want to break free, God invites me to confess and reject prideful dishonesty. I'll be most real and strong if I also tell a trusted friend or two, who can stick with me as I make a change of heart, character and direction.
- I will choose to be up front with someone each day this week. And I will be honest to admit a challenge, mistake, or weakness.

> A man's deepest courage comes from receiving God's view of him—forgiven and affirmed as His beloved son.

Comparing our insides to other people's outsides is stupid.

13

KILL THE FEAR AND PRETENDING

I entered most of my twelve preseasons in the NFL without having a secure spot on the team. I had to prove myself to have any hope of making the roster. That was especially true in a preseason game early in my career when the odds were stacked against me. The Rams put me in to quarterback for one quarter against the San Diego Chargers.

On a third down play, the pocket collapsed, and I scrambled to the right. I was caught from behind by their lightning fast outside linebacker. He picked me up and slammed me headfirst into the turf. I wobbled back to the huddle, oblivious to the fact that it was fourth down and the punt team was in the huddle. Our grizzled star Jack Youngblood chuckled at me, "What are you doing, kid?" He grabbed me by my shoulder pads and guided (shoved) me to the sideline. I passed the *How many fingers?*

concussion protocol (that's the way things were done then) and was sent back in for the next series.

My brain was in full fuzzy mode. I couldn't decipher the play signals from the sideline and winged it for a couple plays. I took the snap and dropped back for a pass but didn't know what routes *any* of the receivers would run. I saw tight end Mike Barber hook up directly in the zone in front of me and threw him the ball. First down. The next pass didn't turn out as well. Again, I had no clue where my receivers would be. When I saw a Charger linebacker appear to be wide open in my line of sight, I instinctively threw it to him for an easy interception.

I walked off the field to our head coach, Ray Malavasi. With a rare lack of insecurity, I said to him, "Coach, I can't think so well."

"That's obvious," he replied. I was benched for the rest of the game.

It's too bad that it took a concussion to make me that honest. It's also too bad that my honesty was as temporary as my concussion. Once my brain recovered, I went back to the familiar ways of acting like I had it all under control.

REAL IS NOT PERFECT

The raw details shared about men in the Bible prove that God isn't looking for flawless character or spotless bios. Though revered as a king, David failed miserably. He didn't always live God's truth, but he did have a heart for it. He was man enough to face the reality about himself, the good, and the horrifically bad. David learned how to fully confess, mourn his offense, repent, apologize, and change his ways. That's what God is looking for. God blesses honesty. That's the path to manhood that's real and good.

> The path to manhood that's real and good is honesty.

Please grasp this: your wounds, your past, your failings, and your flaws don't define or disqualify you—unless you hide behind them. Unless you ignore, deny, pretend, pose, and wall off because of them.

I gained some crucial coaching for manhood from Jim Daly whose traumatic childhood was marked by his dad's abandoning the family, losing his mom to cancer and the fallout of what happened next.

"Another major blow to my emotional concept of manhood occurred when I was nine years old," Jim explains. "My stepdad had just abandoned us, and I was placed in foster care with a family that was emotionally distant and disconnected. Their son stole some things from me. When I reported it to the parents, they didn't take me seriously or even investigate. They said, 'Markey would never do that; you're just not fitting into the family.' After being let down so many times by my father and stepfather, this experience in foster care further solidified my belief that *adults don't tell the truth.*"

For years Jim's outlook on life was centered on believing that "adults don't tell the truth." But it also created in him a hunger for truth. His search led him to consider and receive Christ. A traumatized orphan found his secure identity as a son of a perfect Father.

Jim has become an international leader through the ministry of Focus on the Family. He knows the damage that hiding and running from truth does to men, marriages, families, and generations of children.

Here's what he said about becoming a real and good man:

Each man needs to understand his own reality and how it does or doesn't line up with God's true reality in Scripture. We need to truly know ourselves—our weaknesses as well as our strengths. If we don't know our internal reality, we're like a compass next to a magnet, spinning without direction. We need to know ourselves well and be honest about our "kryptonite," the things that rob us of our honesty, strength, and spiritual vitality. The only way to do that is to engage in earnest self-reflection and to know the Word of God.

Jim's experience is consistent with the pattern we all face. When we operate from our insecurity, we tend to believe lies. Those lies fuel fear in us that creates a perception-based narrative. We then live based on that narrative instead of reality. The key is to figure out the lies so God can obliterate them.

> If you live from a perception-based reality instead of God's declared reality, you will believe lies.

Here are the diamonds of man wisdom I learned from Jim Daly: *know reality, gain self-awareness, live truthfully.*

All of us face insecurity, pressure, anxiety, fear of failure, loneliness, losses, and an exaggerated sense of shame. We have brittle egos, too much self-consciousness, and unhealthy pride. These morph into guardedness, hiding, posing, pretending, and secrecy. This is the fallout of numbing our feelings and putting on a front to look good to others.

On the other side of honesty there is power and freedom for those who face the truth and take humble responsibility for their mistakes, shortcomings, and failures. The greatest leaders have the courage to be vulnerable.

> A man takes humble responsibility for his life and is courageously vulnerable.

How about you? Have you allowed ego and insecurity—fixating on what others might think or say about you—to kill your honesty? Are you hiding things and pretending?

No matter how long you've been holding back the truth, whatever that truth is, there is freedom and momentum in coming clean. The price seems high at the moment but pays off over time. You can become the real you. You can start changing. You can connect and relate to others as the real you.

BEING KNOWN

Being *real* means being *known*. Being known lets you feel more secure, respected, and loved . . . not because you never screw up, but because you're not afraid to confess when you do. Being known requires having appropriate people (not the whole world) know your wounds, weaknesses, struggles, and failures.

My friend Marvin is an exceptional leader with a turnaround story (which I shared in chapter 6). Marvin changed when he received Jesus, resulting in dramatic changes to his marriage, parenting, and leadership. But that didn't give him immunity to traps and secret habits. Because he had developed a struggle with porn, Marvin still needed to turn the corner and become honest and vulnerable. Because that's where the power is.

I asked Marvin what set him free.

"My wife walked in on me watching a pornographic movie. She just turned and walked out. I started panicking like we do when we're caught with our pants down. I felt shame, dishonor, the guilt of betrayal and fear that *my marriage is over; it's all lost*.

"Next morning, she comes in with breakfast, coffee, juice—everything. I'm thinking, 'Wow!'"

"I asked her to sit down and said, 'First of all, I need to apologize for my behavior and for everything I do. I can't even begin to deny it or excuse it. I'm wrong and treated you wrong. I am so sorry and will never do this again.'"

"I had the confidence to say that because I knew God was at work. It was God's grace that caused her to catch me, walk away without reacting, and then serve me breakfast. I knew it was a miracle of grace from God. Even though I had veered off the trail, I knew this was an opportunity to get back on the trail, the right road, and quit. I've not even come close to doing it again."

that the best way to live his new life was in total honesty. He knew that Christ set him free, but in his first years as a Christian, he held back on telling his whole story, including the part about pornography. A pastor had discouraged transparency about his past lifestyle and present struggles. Marvin wasn't at peace with that approach but went along with the advice. That changed at a men's retreat when he heard a man freely lay out the messy stuff in his heart—all of it.

Marvin's response was, "I *knew* you could do that. I *knew* you didn't need to hide. I got in a group with that guy. Those guys helped me know that God desires, enjoys, and honors truth. Honesty became real for me"

WE ALL NEED HELP

I hope you've already begun to internalize what I'm about to share, but I need to make sure.

God can handle you being real. He doesn't want you to hide from Him—which you can't do anyway. God already knows it all. His Holy Spirit is prompting you to disclose and confess all that stuff that you've been—stuffing—to Abba Father so that His forgiveness can heal and set you free.

Jesus came and lived with the same temptations and pain we face so that he could forgive all our failing and conquer all our struggles.

I believe God wants you to be crystal clear on these things. You don't need to act as though things are okay when they're not. You can admit to Him what's messed up, or not making sense to you.

God hasn't lost control. His grand plan does not fail. He's always working in all situations for His ultimate glory. He turns suffering into spiritual riches, tragedy into triumph, and evil into justice. The limitations of our smaller perspective don't stop His benevolence and justice.

You are never, ever alone. Just as Father God was with Jesus when he was rejected on earth, He is with us in every moment and situation. He was even with you in your worst trauma or ugliest infidelity. His same power that forgives, saves, and adopts you as His son is also available to help you. If you put your whole life and every situation in His hands, He'll empower you to live His way instead of your way. He wants you to know that so that you don't drift from His presence and help.

Honesty and total disclosure with God invites His healing transformation. Jesus already paid the full punishment for everything we could ever do wrong. So, accept the invitation and forgiveness and move into full honesty. Jesus paid the highest price for it. Be real with God. Get real and stay honest with a couple of quality friends. That will strengthen your confession and accelerate your transformation and freedom from the junk you've been stuck in.*

Hopefully we have at least a flicker of conscience about the ways we pretend. That discomfort in our conscience is a good thing. We need to remind ourselves that we gain more peace, more progress, and more authentic and enjoyable relationships when we're honest about who we are.

Here's the question I try to ask often: Am I making the courageous effort to be real?

Break that question down further and it looks like this:

Do I:

- pretend to be nicer than I am?
- cut corners or compromise when no one is looking?
- inflate my work, accomplishments, and activities to impress others?

---

* My thanks to Paul David Tripp for inspiration from his book, *New Morning Mercies: A Daily Gospel Devotional* (Crossway Books, 2014). I'm also drawing from Jesus' words found in John 16:32-33.

- give the impression I don't struggle with problems and vices like others do?
- take credit for other people's ideas or insights?
- make my motives sound unselfish when they're not?
- keep secrets from others—my wife, friends, boss?

If you and I want to be set free from this wearying charade—If you want to get to a place where you feel accepted and loved for who you actually are—If you want your relationships with God, family, and friends to be healthy—you can get there.

Just not on your own.

But, by going to God and seeking His help, you can.

We're all broken souls with blind spots in our personality and compromises in our character. We'd be better off to just admit it. This would allow us to receive the freedom and healing of God's forgiveness.

> The one who trusts in himself *(keeping his struggles and decisions to himself)* is a fool, but one who walks in wisdom *(in honesty, disclosure, and counsel)* will be safe.
> —Proverbs 28:26 (HCSB)

We all have our insecurities and particular fears. We don't want to be thought of as a failure. Please remember that Father God alone provides the answer to those dilemmas. The answer is found in centering your life securely in Jesus and living in intentional, consistent, and honest relationships with friends who live the same way.

Invite God to help you kill the fear and pretending. Being real and known is far better.

ASK MYSELF

- "What dominant thing do I yearn for and think I need to feel good about myself—my idol?"

MY ACTIONS

- I will talk with God openly about what He already knows and can handle. I will confess it all and let Him disarm my lie, dethrone my idol and defeat my pattern of sin.
- I will deepen my honesty and power to change by sharing with a close friend or a few trusted friends. I will share my story with them, including stuff I've been hiding. If I have trauma or addictive behavior, I will also see a professional counselor, who believes in the grace and power of Christ.

We don't live by reality, but by subjective perceptions and false narratives. Those are shaped by fear. Fear is lit by the devil's lies. Fear kills trust in God. Fear fuels reactive living as we self-protect and self-promote. This is a concept from Jamie Winship which I've amplified.

"We can't afford to be afraid of what we fear."
—U2, Red Flag Day

"Real confidence comes from God, not ourselves."
—David Robbins

HUDDLE

14

FRIENDS & MENTORS

Friendship is a treasure. Unfortunately, for many of us it's a hidden treasure because we invest so little in it. So little time. So little attention. So little of ourselves.

Friendship is the very thing that caused Sandy and his newlywed wife Sue to write a $400 check to Arthur, Sandy's best friend. It was an act of love that left them with exactly four dollars in their checking account.

You read that right—four dollars. Here's the story.

Sandy's family was Jewish. His parents escaped Nazi Germany in 1939 and eventually settled in Buffalo, New York. When Sandy was five, his father died, leaving his mom with three children and fifty-four dollars. She worked hard to overcome poverty and to raise Sandy and his two siblings. Eventually, she found love again and remarried.

As he grew, Sandy excelled academically. He became class president in high school and earned an academic scholarship to Columbia

University where, in his freshman year he met another Jewish kid named Arthur.

Sandy and Arthur decided to room together. As their friendship developed, Arthur suggested they make a pact that "if either was ever in real need, the other would have his back."

In the years that followed, both men would live up to that promise.

In his junior year, Sandy was misdiagnosed with glaucoma and the treatment he was given caused him to go blind. This resulted in his reluctantly agreeing with his parents that dropping out of Columbia was the best thing to do since he could no longer navigate the sidewalks of New York City.

Soon, Arthur flew to Buffalo to visit Sandy and his family. "I'm here to persuade you to come back," Arthur told him. "It's not so much that you have to come back for yourself, though you do. But I need you there. You're my best friend, aren't you?" He then reminded Sandy of their pact and promised to take Sandy to his classes and read his coursework to him.

Sandy would later attribute Arthur's commitment and generosity as the key to overcoming his crisis, walking with him through darkness. Arthur even referred to himself as "Darkness" when he read to Sandy. It was his way of reminding Sandy that he was with him in his dark and sightless world. "Darkness" was Sandy's friend.

As good friends sometimes do, Arthur pushed Sandy. In Sandy's first semester as a blind man, Arthur took him downtown to a social service agency near Grand Central Station in Manhattan. He then told Sandy that he couldn't return to the Columbia campus just then, so Sandy would have to make it back on his own. Sandy describes it as the most harrowing two hours of his life. He was weary and a little bruised after making the journey, and just as he was arriving at his apartment building, a man bumped into him.

"Excuse me, sir," the man said. Immediately Sandy recognized the voice; it was Arthur. He had been shadowing Sandy the whole time.

A couple years after graduation, their roles reversed. Sandy was a newlywed and studying at Oxford University in England. Arthur mentioned to Sandy that he needed $400 to record a musical album with Paul, one of his musician buddies. Though Sandy and his wife's checking account had only $404 in it, the memories of Arthur reading to him for countless hours immediately prompted him to write a $400 check and send it to Arthur.

Arthur, who had started going by Art, recorded a song on that album that eventually became a hit. The first line of the song had special meaning to Sandy: "Hello Darkness, my old friend." Art parlayed Sandy's $400 investment into another partnership of friends, teaming with Paul Simon to record Simon & Garfunkel's hit song, "The Sound of Silence."*

Friendships don't have to result in magnificent achievements or fame to have value. Committing to friends—to connect consistently, to have one another's backs, to encourage, to give and receive—will make us better men. It will open up positive parts of life that we would otherwise miss.

A significant friendship doesn't just make us feel good about ourselves, overlooking our errors and affirming

> A significant friendship validates you, gives you confidence you can grow, and refuses to leave you unchanged.

* Brady, Erik (2014, December 20). Sandy Greenberg's Quest for Sight Found Solace and Hope in Darkness His Old Friend. The Buffalo News. https://buffalonews.com/opinion/columnists/erik-brady-sandy-greenbergs-quest-for-sight-found-solace-and-hope-in-darkness-his-old/article_946f2f5e-3bd7-11eb-9649-077c32876846.html.

our biases. A significant friendship is valuable because it validates us, gives us confidence that we can grow, and refuses to leave us unchanged. Being our true self with a true friend helps us see ourselves more accurately, who we really are and who we can become. It makes us more self-aware, which is crucial to tackling life wisely.

Let's pick up a few tips and chew on what I'm learning about friendship from a couple of quality friends, teammates, and mentors.

CHARLIE

I switched from a large public high school with good football and great academics to a slightly larger public high school with great football and great academics. I went from being a small fish in a big pond to being a tiny minnow in a bigger pond. I was intimidated by the older football players and students, but I had a friend on my street who was a senior and a starter on the team, a guy named Charlie Marck.

Charlie was cool. He was accepted. I was neither. We became workout buddies. We ran miles and sprints and threw the football at our high school field during the summers of our high school and college years. Charlie and I were working together on something that was important to both of us. Even so, our friendship was probably more valuable to me than to him because I was younger, new to the team and school, and needed the sense of belonging. Being Charlie's friend gave me the endorsement I was looking for.

We're still friends today. When we talk on the phone or connect in person, we joke like we used to, but quickly open up and talk about the real and important stuff. We pray for each other. Even though the visible evidence of our faith was sparse back then, we both knew the other guy desired a strong faith and that common bond helped us both grow.

Doing things together that matter to you both can forge deep friendships.

TOM

Tom Flick is an introvert. I'm an extrovert. He's a detail and method guy who maps things out and executes them well. I'm a dreamer with a lot of spontaneity. Tom and I have a few shared interests, including biking, skiing, and being outdoors, and one very special thing: faith in Christ.

After retiring from football, the routine of constantly being around buddies ended. Tom was the first guy I decided to get together with regularly for intentional weekly conversations about life. We processed stuff we were

> Significant friendships demand consistency in getting together.

going through, ideas we had, things we were learning, and things we wanted to understand. We prayed for each other and each other's families. We were clear about the trust and confidential nature of our relationship. We aimed to be open books. We admitted our flaws and temptations, processed our motives, and disarmed life-killing secrets.

As simple as it sounds, the strength of our friendship grew through our consistency in getting together. I believe that if we had stopped meeting regularly, honest disclosure would have been harder. Our private struggles would have overgrown our good intentions and created gaps in our friendship and character.

If you want a great friendship, start connecting consistently. Aim for openness. Define your purpose, commit to confidentiality, and stick with it.

I think a lot of men are lonely. Their network may be huge, and lives might appear fully loaded with work, events, trips, and hobbies. But the hectic pace isn't giving them what their heart truly needs: friendship.

There are a lot of guys in your neighborhood, at work, and even in church who feel that way. Maybe you're one of them.

You could keep waiting for a friend to show up and step into your life. Or you could step into theirs as a friend.

MENTORING

Figuring out manhood can be confusing unless manhood is developed among other mature men. I strongly encourage you to add another layer to your friendships by seeking a mentor.

CHUCK

Chuck Obremski was my best friend. I met him when he was a thirty-year-old entrepreneur who had worked his way into owning his own heating and air-conditioning company in Southern California. He had a wife, three young kids, a Pittsburgh accent, a blue-collar lexicon, and a knack for explaining the Bible—especially to the interested players of the Los Angeles Rams, California Angels, and Anaheim Mighty Ducks.

Chuck chose to be my friend. He invested time and effort in me. He cared. He talked to me about everything, but always with God and His Word as the foundation of whatever we discussed. Chuck changed my relationship with God. He also changed my leadership, my husbanding, my fathering, my goals, and my approach to friendship.

Chuck loved me, laughed with me, cried with me, hung out with me, mentored me and discipled me. He did it all as a friend who became my mentor.

We had only a few in-person years together, and a few additional ones by phone. Chuck died after an exuberant and gutsy eighteen-month battle with myeloma. He viewed his cancer as an opportunity to show people that life in God's family transcends circumstances in this short life.

Chuck went overboard to help my family as I was traded around the NFL. His mentoring was way more than our conversations and the wisdom he passed along to me. The way he faced the ravaging blitz of cancer with more joy and energy than anyone I've ever seen is the greatest influence he had. When he passed, 3,000 people came to Angels Stadium in Anaheim for his memorial service.

If you really appreciate what God has done to love, forgive, and welcome you into His better life and bigger kingdom, you will hunger to know what He has to say to you in His Word. The transforming power of life in Christ will generate passion and bandwidth to care for others, be with them, serve them, mentor, and teach them what you're learning.

> You need to get off the sidelines and seek out a mentor who knows the Lord and will help you process what's going on in your life.

My challenge to you is to get off the sidelines—if that's where you're hanging out right now. Get connected with God's men. Go ask a good man, a man who knows God, to mentor you. Ask him for stories and lessons from his life. Ask if you can process stuff going on in your life. Ask Him for stories from his life and for wisdom from God and His Word.

Just get started. Don't overthink it. A mentor can be with you for a long season of life, or he can meet with you just a few times over coffee.

There are all kinds of mentorship. I just want you to see it as a natural, elemental aspect to manhood. You know about mentorship for career building and skill development, but I want you to know it as a central part of the teamwork of manhood, faith, marriage and being a dad.

> Don't disqualify yourself as a mentor; step up and give to others what you have received.

One more thing—don't disqualify yourself from *being* a mentor. Remember how vital teamwork is—which means you need friends, and they need you. Someday, maybe today, you'll need to step up and give to others what you have received.

Be mentored. Be mentoring.

ASK MYSELF

- "If we talked often about our lives, what friend and what possible mentor would encourage my faith and help me be a better man, husband or dad?"

MY ACTIONS

- I will call that guy(s) this week to catch up, laugh at a memory and show I'm interested in how he's doing.
- I will ask what's been good lately and what's been tough—and be quick to share my tough stuff.

"Every man needs three kinds of friends—a Paul, a Barnabas & a Timothy. A Paul who can mentor and challenge him; a Barnabas who can come alongside him, live life together and encourage him; and a Timothy who h2e can pour his life into and mentor."

—**Howard Hendricks**

15

LEVEL 5 FRIENDS HUDDLE

M ike Woodruff ran a robust college ministry for many years. Today he's a pastor, Christian leader, and author. He's always had an extensive network and lots of "friends." Even so, he'll tell you that early in his career, his life was full but thin.

Two years into his marriage, Mike's wife Sheri wanted to help him shore up a weak part of his life. She saw a gap and pointed it out: "You don't have any friends, and sadder than that, you don't even realize it."

Mike was stung by her assessment.

He countered, "Friends! I've got so many I can't even keep track of them."

Mike went on to do what I would have done, and maybe you would have too, he began naming the many friends he'd had in school, college, and career, as well as w guys he'd met through various activities.

"Those are not actual friends," Sheri replied. "That's not the way it works. Friends are people you spend time with, and who know what is really going on in your life."

Sheri was letting Mike know that there are various "levels" of friends, but real friends have depth. Let's go beyond your network—the casual, basic, and "pretty good" friends you have. Let's talk about the best of friendship, deep friendship. We'll call it "Level 5 Friendship."

> "76% of men don't have a close and trusted friend they can share anything with on any topic."
> —2021 Perspectives Survey by The Survey Center on American Life

LEVEL 5 FRIENDSHIP

Friendship wasn't invented or mastered without its author, Jesus. He's the source for the best of friendship. But the idea of Level 5 Friendship was sparked for me by a principle in Jim Collins' bestselling business book *Good to Great* about effective leadership that led to transformation and greatness in their enterprise. Collins observed the performance of elite business leaders, and their inner qualities. Level 5 leaders were the most influential because they surpassed all others in combining two key traits: humility and focus. They were genuinely humble and kept their team focused on the one main thing.

> Level 5 Friendship hinges on humility and intentionality.

Just as the type and impact of leadership varies, so does friendship. Some friendships are far more influential and life-giving than others. Many guys have not cultivated any friendships past the "good friend" stage—level 3. They may have many of them, but they're missing something vital and rich, something intentional you can only have with a few guys.

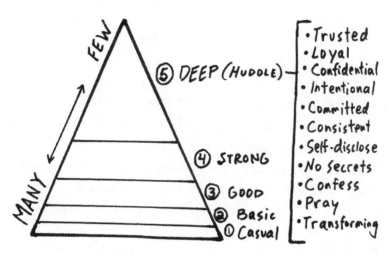

Before you ask, no, I don't keep score of my friendships, moving guys up and down the scale depending on how well we're getting along or what they've done for me lately. I'm simply pointing out that we can have—and need to have—some stronger and deeper friendships that make us better men. Your mind is likely jumping ahead to, *"What's a Level 4 and Level 5 Friend?"*

A *Level 4 Friend* is a guy you'd call at 2am. You know each other well. You've been through some intense things together. You've shared some scars, victories and secrets. He's a guy you trust and can open up with. He's a strong, dependable buddy—but you may not connect often or know what's going on in real time. That means you can't help each other week to week on the most important stuff going on. He's not Level 5.

> A Level 5 Friend is intentional, committed, and consistent. His friendship is transforming, moving me from AS IS toward TO BE.

A Level 5 Friend is more than strong, dependable and valued. He's intentional, committed, and consistent. You've defined your friendship as consistent connecting, trusting loyalty, and open honesty as you process your lives together. *Level 5 Friendship* is *transforming*. It moves us along from *AS IS* toward *TO BE*.

My gut tells me that the guys we would put on our "Level 5 Prospect List" (no, I don't have one of those either) feel the same desire for deep friendship as we do. There are men out there, maybe some who are already in your circle, who are humble enough to know they need consistency and vulnerability with a couple of close friends, gutsy enough to commit to self-disclosure, and self-aware enough to know they need to connect consistently in order to process the key issues of life.

> Level 5 Friends schedule time together to HUDDLE for great purpose and depth.

Intentionality is the main characteristic that sets Level 5 Friendship at the top. We're not talking about the guy you'd consider a buddy, or even a close friend. We're talking about two or three friends that literally schedule time together for great purpose and depth. That's huddling. This consistent gathering is the action of Level 5 friendship. It's a verb. You can call your meeting a huddle or even call your tight group of gathering friends your huddle.

More about that in a minute. For now, let's pick back up with Mike and Sheri.

Mike held his ground for a few weeks, insisting that he had plenty of friends. But the more he thought about it, the more he realized Sheri was right. So, he *intentionally* set out to forge some real friendships. Which he did.

Decades later, Mike still talks on the phone with two of those men a few times each week. It's usually not a long conversation, and like any friendship, they joke around some (Level Five doesn't mean Zero Fun!).

But they always get to the really important stuff: what struggles they're in, what decisions they're facing, what temptations they're battling. At least once a year, they get together in person for some adventure and a deep friendship dive. They even created a preparation tool for their annual get-together.*

YOUR HUDDLE

A huddle on the football field is the place for teammates to come together to communicate a shared plan to help them win. If players don't connect and align assignments, the game is already lost. Am I right?

We could say the same about life, where there's much more at stake. A man, on his own, without support, without the accountability of a shared game plan—that man is in for trouble. And he's missing out on the best of friendship!

A men's Huddle is a tight group of three or four friends who meet regularly to help each other. Each man is accepted and supported as he processes life in the company of brothers who care as much for him as they do for themselves. Ideally, it's a brotherhood that chooses to live in the light with one another and to become more like Jesus.

A Huddle has these characteristics:

- Trusting, Confidential & Loyal—The huddle is always, always a safe place to open up, discuss, and pray about the most important things going on in each man's life. No hiding. No secrets.
- Defined Purpose—The purpose of huddling is clearly stated and understood by each man: to help one another live honestly, deal with the past and to move forward in becoming the men Christ invites them to be.

---

* You can see Mike's gameplan for friendship in his book *Friends for the Broken* on his website at www.mikewoodruff.org

- Consistency—Each man is intentional and committed to meet regularly with his friend team. He makes connecting a high priority. He knows he needs to both give and receive dependability, to be there for his brothers and they for him.
- Transformative—The huddle atmosphere invites self-disclosure, increases self-awareness, and supports spiritual growth. It adds wisdom and prevents doing dumb stuff. It moves us forward in faith, character and relationships.
- Fun—A tight-knit team of deep friends enjoy laughter, empathy, and mutual support.

Think back to the closest friendships of your past, when hanging out with your buddies was comfortable and you could talk about almost anything that was on your mind. You're at a different stage of life now, and maybe you've had to leave some of those friendships behind for various reasons. Even so, you *still* need solid friendships. Truth be told, you might need them now more than you ever have. But again, it will take intentionality on your part to connect and develop some Level 5 Friends. There are proven ways to do this. A great start is defining the type of friendship you're hoping to build with a couple of men.*

Isn't this what Jesus did?

Jesus showed up differently than most people in Israel expected Him to. Not coming on the scene as an all-star politician or religious mega-leader, He took on the role of a village carpenter instead. He made friends with average guys, including a few professional fishermen, a young doctor, and

---

* You can find coaching and tips for growing deep friendships and starting a huddle in our *Level 5 Friendship Playbook*. Download it free at www.menhuddle .com.

a despised tax collector. He invited them to be His friends and He took them into deeper levels of friendship with one another.

Jesus went especially deep with Peter, James, and John, bringing them in on special experiences, like healing a religious leader's daughter and joining Him on a mountain to witness His transfiguration.

He hung out with these men, ate with them, and visited them at work. He traveled with them—on foot and on the water. He involved them in what He was doing. He took them away for times of camaraderie and rest. He let them in on His secrets. He explained His mission and briefed them on His ultimate plan.

> 2,000 years after Jesus and His friends began changing the world, no strategy or method has replaced deep friendship. It's the root system that nourishes growth and sustains life change.

Jesus also tackled their personal issues head-on. Several days after He was raised to life, He cooked breakfast for Peter who had denied Him three times in a crucial hour. Jesus hadn't given up on Peter. He lifted him back up with triple-forgiving assurance and a triple-affirming assignment.

Two thousand years after Jesus and His friends began to spread the message of faith in Christ, the role of deep friendship has never been improved on. It is the root system that nourishes growth and sustains life change. In reality, few men will make and sustain any significant change in life without a viable team of supportive friends or mentors. A small percentage of men will come to church events and programs. Events and programs can positively impact, but God's men truly come alive through deep friendship, which Jesus demonstrated.

As the greatest leader ever, Jesus began to change the world through these few men that He called *friends* (see John 15:14-17). His way of deep friendship is a model for all of us, but especially for those who represent

Him in leadership roles. Leaders show the way for other men, but they also face increased risks of isolation and ego-driven compromise. Leaders especially need the grounding of deep and transparent friendship.

If that's you, and you want men to benefit from deep friendship, you need to live it yourself. Deep down, it's what you want, anyway.

I've seen what can happen when guys experience teamwork and the iron-sharpening-iron strength of other men. When we live out friendship this way, we are doing it the Jesus way.

Greg and Pete are the two friends I huddle with every Tuesday evening at 5:15. We used to walk and talk on a trail by the river and even met in Pete's pool on some sweltering nights. We meet by Zoom now since Greg moved to another state. Often, we switch the evening or time so we can stay consistent when our family needs us, or our schedules change.

> Leadership can isolate. I need deep friendship, especially as I face increased risks of isolation and ego-driven compromise.

When we huddle each week, we do a quick Self X-Ray of our life and ask three questions:

1. What's the most important thing you need to talk about?
2. What's most important for me to pray for you?
3. What's Father God saying to you (as you read His Word and talk with Him)?

We've been doing this for nine years now. We know all about one another's family, jobs, personal strengths and weaknesses. We know each other's likes, quirks, risk-areas and bad behavior. I'm sure we do much less dumb stuff as husbands, dads, and men than we would if we weren't connected in this way. Some of that is because we run ideas by each other in our weekly huddle. Some of it is because we're committed to telling the truth about what's going on in our lives and admitting our temptations and slip-ups. We also live better by getting some good ideas from each other as we process our lives openly, with a commitment to honesty and confidentiality.

Here's a day in the life of an imperfect guy with Level 5 Friendship.

After a long day of speaking at a men's conference out of town, I came back to my hotel and plopped down on my bed. Instead of getting some much-needed sleep, I was distracted by the couple in the room next door. They were neither reserved nor quiet as they had sex. I didn't slip on my noise-canceling headphones or turn up the TV volume. I kept the TV off, tuned into the couple and fed my sexual curiosity.

It was auditory porn, but no harm in accidentally hearing it. My compromise was tuning into it and listening with lustful imagination. I even checked the next night to see if they were at it again. I realized my compromise needed to stop before it recurred or spread, so I could stay free and loyal to God, Stacy, and myself. To end it, I had to kill the secret.

I had a commitment to myself (and my wife) that I'd come clean with my temptations and failures as soon as I could share them with my huddle amigos. I already had a lunch scheduled with Pete for Monday. Pete's a great guy, humble, cheerful and truly loves God, his wife and his family. I couldn't imagine Pete messing up as I just had with my sexual curiosity and imagination. I was not relishing telling him about my weakness and compromise on a weekend where I was coaching men on faith and loyalty.

I told myself that before allowing myself any chips and salsa, I'd tell Pete about it. Man! It went so much better than my insecurity (and the devil) had convinced me it would. Instead of rolling his eyes, frowning, looking down or shaking his head at me, Pete smiled and leaned toward me. He thanked me for my honesty and brightened up as he told me that he especially appreciated my openness and honesty.

We all fear losing respect in situations like this. But Pete's response was like a fresh breeze clearing it away. Instead, I felt a wave of unexpected respect coming from him. After affirming me for being humble and forthright, Pete thanked me and swiftly unloaded a small secret compromise he'd been caving in to for the last couple of weeks. My self-disclosure and confession triggered his respect and his own disclosure and confession.

Pete and I had experienced the power of horizontal confession. As we started pounding the chips, we were not at all feeling like secret-keeping hypocrites or losers. We felt accepted, free, and invigorated. We walked away much stronger to face future temptations with prayer support from a friend and the peer-to-peer accountability of living in the light, not in secrecy.

God made our souls desire connection and belonging. When we take fear and image-protecting out of a friendship, powerful things happen, but only if we open up and disclose what's really going on.

CS Lewis was a man of friendships and saw it this way: "Friendship . . . is born at the moment when one man says to another "What! You too? I thought that no one but myself . . ."

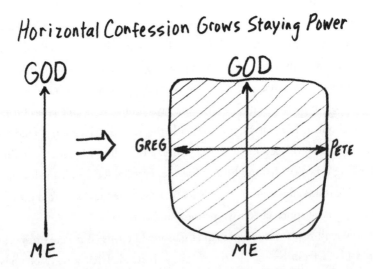

Horizontal Confession Grows Staying Power

Believe me, Pete and Greg help me live a better life. I want you to have a deep connection with friends like we do.

Now, if you're skeptical about creating this level of friendship, I understand. And I would agree that what I've described is unlikely to happen for you—if—you keep doing things the same way you've been doing them. But, if you're willing to be intentional with a few guys, and if you define trusting one another, you've got a good start. Scheduling a weekly call with a simple question is a discipline every guy can execute. Deep friendship, like everything else good, will come when we ask Father God to lead us and receive it from Him.

And if you're ready to create deeper friendship, download *Level 5 Friendship Playbook* at www.menhuddle.com to share with a couple of buddies.

ASK MYSELF

- "What's holding me back from having a couple of deep and consistent friendships? How do I plan to overcome that?"

MY ACTIONS

- I will ask God to help me pick two friends to call weekly to stay current and go deeper. I will check in weekly with a call to ask them, "What's the most important thing you need to talk about?" I will be quick to open up and share my important stuff.
- I will download and print the *Level 5 Friendship Playbook* (www.men huddle.com). And I'll share it with a couple friends to start a dialogue about getting intentional and consistent with our friendship and huddling.

"As iron sharpens iron, a friend sharpens a friend."
—Proverbs 27:17 NLT

"And let us consider how we may spur one another on toward love and good deeds, not giving up meeting together, as some are in the habit of doing, but encouraging one another . . ."
—Hebrews 10:24-25

"Share each other's burdens; and in this way obey the law of Christ."
—Galatians 6:2 NLT

"But if we are living in the light, as God is in the light, then we have fellowship with each other, and the blood of Jesus, his Son, cleanses us from all sin."
—1 John 1:7 NLT

A VITAL DISTINCTION

Are you curious why I didn't mention men's groups, small groups and accountability groups? It's because I'm emphasizing friendship, the Way of Jesus. I'm a huge supporter of all those valuable groups which can offer men seasons of teamwork, training and encouragement. BUT, unlike friendship or brotherhood, groups can be joined and un-joined. Groups will only be as deep and effective as the trust and friendships. Transformative friendship is the key—Level 5—with loyalty, depth and consistency. That's why I'm emphasizing the action verb of friendship, huddling.

16

LIVE IN THE GAME PLAN

See if you track with me so far. The journey to be a real and good man starts with realizing that Jesus was the only fully real and good man. He is our model, fully authentic and always beneficial for others. You receive your identity as an accepted, valued son of Father God through trusting faith in Jesus Christ. God has a purpose for your life: to become like Jesus. His plan and provision for you is to receive guidance and strength from Him, huddle with brothers, transform in character, and lift other people and situations to the best that God intends.

God has communicated His plan through the way Jesus lived and through God's Word, the Bible. This game plan is the same for every person He created. What's unique to us as individuals is the specific pathway He takes us on through our relationship with Christ and the life-shaping power of Scripture.

If you ask Him, He'll show you how to relate to Him well. My goal is to help you experience this by: (1) approaching God as *Father*, and (2) interacting with the Bible as a dialogue with your Father concerning every moment and issue of your life.

> God has communicated His plan through the way Jesus lived and through His Word.

God invites you to develop an attitude and posture toward Him as your Father who already forgives, accepts, loves, and affirms you before you change anything. Your approach becomes all about relating to your perfect Father so that you can live the inspired life and empowered mission He designed for you.

Think about the Scriptures as *the* game plan for your life—spiritually alive and dynamic—to transform and guide you. Read the Bible as a son who expects to hear his Father speak.

OUR PLAYBOOK

My NFL teams had a 4-inch-thick playbook for the season. Our coaches developed each week's game plan from the playbook, tailoring it to our players and what we knew about our opponents. The best players internalized the game plan because they loved to excel and win. They understood that mastering it empowered them to play with freedom and excellence.

The playbook is crucial, but it only helps you if you immerse yourself in it and internalize it. Then you execute it. The purpose of the playbook isn't to pass a test; it's a dynamic plan to help a team win.

ENGAGING WITH THE COACH

How we engage with God and with the Bible becomes much more meaningful and impactful when we view it within the *relationship* we have with our Father.

Imagine walking into an NFL team's quarterbacks' meeting expecting to get the game plan for an upcoming championship game. You expect to be handed a tablet with lists of plays, diagrams, coaching tips and video clips that describe the strategy and show the actual plays being run. But instead—

Your head coach walks in the room. He's unlike any other coach in the league. He's a phenomenal coach, and he's also the team owner. He's also a former player, and he's managed to keep himself in optimal physical and mental condition. He knows everything about you as a player, including your thoughts. One thing that matters most to him: that you respect him.

You're eager to learn from him and so you're committed to do whatever he coaches you to do. He responds to your respect and goes beyond just giving you the game plan.

He's not normal; He's supernatural. He teleports Himself into your body. He implants His knowledge of the game plan into your understanding. He fills your body with His ability. He turbocharges your motivation with His more noble motives. As a result, your confidence surges. You're filled with peace because He guarantees that the season, no matter how difficult, will end with a championship.

> Approaching God as my Father opens me up to what He is going to say to me.

Wild metaphor, right? But you get the point. I think it's a more accurate picture of how a man can live with Father God and His Word than many of the pictures we've seen because the coach enters, transforms, and empowers the player. The key to living an overcoming life as a man is *receiving* Father God's game plan for your life and letting *Him* live it out *through* you—something you could never do in your own strength.

I've tried to read, study, memorize, and been taught the Bible for much of my life, but it's never been as exciting and alive to me as it has been in the last three years. Why? Because I've started approaching God as my Father and reading Scripture as listening to what my Father is going to say to me.

ON MISSION

Jesus got direction and guidance from His Father. He went to His Father, listened to His Father, and got the clarity and power He needed to accomplish His assignment, His mission. The Father intends it to be the same for us.

If you're not connecting to and hearing from Father God in His Word, you'll forget essential things, such as:

- You are His son.
- His love for you is based on grace, which means His forgiveness, acceptance, and approval come to you because of what Christ did, not your ability to earn them.
- The best of life can only come by trusting God since He alone is perfect and in control.

> I am most like Jesus when I join God's mission and live my calling each day.

You've been given a significant place in God's mission, a calling for here and now, and a place in God's eternal kingdom, which will transcend anything that formerly felt significant or positive in this life.

God gives a man his identity. He gives him a purpose that means living for a cause greater than himself. He lives "on mission." In any job, pursuit or relationship. A man is most like Jesus when he joins God's mission and lives out his calling each day like Jesus did.

APPROACHING THE FATHER

Here are some of the ways that I'm learning to approach God as a son approaches his Father.

- I start the day with Him instead of my phone which immediately distracts me. I try to remain quiet for two minutes. I often say, "Father God, take control of me and my day for Your purposes. Remind me to live as Your son and receive from You everything I feel, think, pray, speak and do today."
- Sometimes I take a walk just to talk with the Father. I thank Him for who He is, for His presence and blessings, and then I tell Him what's troubling me. I also pray for others.
- When I'm reading or studying the Bible, or using a devotion book, I ask the Father what He wants to say to me. I highlight words and phrases that speak to me, and put bullet points in the margins for messages, principles, or prayers He gives me.
- I use a journal to ask God questions and I wait for His response. I often draw a box around each question and prayer I'm waiting for an answer to.

These spiritual habits, the big ones and the small ones, support a basic mindset that aims to think constantly about Jesus. I want to celebrate His love and God's adopting me into His eternal kingdom. I want my vision and hope set on Christ. I want to see Him, thank Him, talk to Him, learn from Him, and become like Him. That's my version of living with Him living in me. It's uniting with Jesus—trusting, thinking and operating with Him. It's abiding in Him.

Jesus said, "I am the vine; you are the branches. If you remain (*connect with, depend upon, receive from*) in me and I in you, you will bear much fruit; apart from me you can do nothing." (John 15:5). Here's my paraphrase:

I, Jesus, am your complete source of life and you are attached to me so that My life, love, and truth can flow into you and through you. When you stay connected and dependent upon Me, I'll develop good thoughts, emotions, plans, words, actions, responses, character, and relationships through everything you do. I'll work through your life to generate positive influence and eternal impact. Just remember that when you do things on your own without Me, you cannot handle life or do anything that counts.

LIFE WITH THE WORD OF GOD

What's important for setting yourself up for the day? Coffee? Breakfast? A run or workout? A charged phone? To be left alone? We view those things as important, so we do our best to get them. And they're fine, but how do they compare with a daily experience that's empowering, supernatural, and transformative?

What about your soul? Does it need to be refreshed and built up? How about your mindset, your attitudes, your perspective? What will really help your relationships thrive with joy, starting with the Father who created and saved you?

I encourage you to take a fresh view of the Bible as your opportunity to hear from Father God. Ask Him to bring His Word alive as the start-up to your day and the regular reset of your life. Planting the Word in your mind in the morning, or any time for that matter, changes the script of your life. It reminds you that your amazingly good Father is in control. It will expose your blind spots and prompt you to confess and apologize for sins. The Word is the wisdom and truth of Jesus that sets you free from sin and addictions. It helps you quit the selfish stuff that trips you up. It'll spur you to put love into action.

CHUCK'S EXAMPLE

*Who do you most respect? Who's been your best friend? Who's faced life's bru-
tal blitz with the most courage and joy while lifting other people? Whose life
has been most magnificently impacted by knowing God through the Bible?*

My answers to those questions all came from the same dude. Chuck
Obremski. He died of cancer at 48 and he changed more men's lives
than any guy I know. His manhood was like Jesus'. He received, transformed, huddled and lifted God and others up. I attribute it all to one
main thing—he lived in God's game plan. He loved Jesus by loving and
digesting God's Word.

Chuck was turned off to church and God when he married his preg-
nant girlfriend. He gave up college and started working for HVAC entre-
preneurs who were Christians. They loved their wives well and treated
employees, clients and vendors ethically and generously.

Chuck had to ask, "What makes you act like this?" Their answer?
"Following Jesus and the Bible."

Chuck's stereotype of Christians broke. So did his resistance to God.
He received Christ and was thrilled to gain life's true answers in the Bible.
He was hungry for God and His wisdom. God fed his hunger.

"The more Chuck studied," his wife Linda said, "the more he changed."
She felt God transform Chuck's heart to love and care for her. His
anger ended. He radically changed into an encouraging dad.

His whole life turned around. He apologized to and forgave his family who had belittled and rejected him. He started memorizing Scripture
and could quickly and naturally bring it into any conversation with anyone. He was fearless and all about love.

He discovered so much in the Bible about His Heavenly Father, his
identity, security, confidence, his work and relationships. It gave him a
compelling mission as a small business owner using his gifts and energies

to help others know God through His Word. Because he'd seen the Bible so change his life, Chuck huddled privately with me and many men so we could discover God's love, put Him first, and learn to study and apply God's truth from the Bible.

Chuck cracked jokes, worked hard and made money. But he treated the Bible as golden treasure—a perfect game plan for every situation and relationship in life: negotiating an NFL contract, getting cut, handling a rotten coach or a dating relationship, dealing with a devastating injury, helping a husband learn to cherish and apologize to his wife. It shows us how to love people and use money. It shows us how to follow Jesus, whether running a business or fearlessly beating a blitz—even one that kills your body.

Chuck preached sermons every week for a year and a half with a weekly schedule of chemo every Monday. He'd be sick till Thursday, study the Bible till Saturday, teach it on Sunday. Chemo again on Monday. On the last Sunday of his life, he was down 60 pounds. Hair gone. Gaunt. And full of more joy than anyone else.

He began his last sermon with typical humor. Sitting in a low chair on stage, he pointed to his oxygen tank with the tube up his nose, the morphine drip I-V on the other side and the study Bible in front of him. "OK, everybody," Chuck grinned, "Get ready. I've got oxygen, I've got morphine, and I've God's almighty word. This sermon could take all day!"

Chuck exuberantly received God's Word and was radically transformed by it. His treasure was in heaven, and he beat his blitz of cancer. It killed his body, but his exuberant soul went to heaven—and thousands will be going there too because of the way Chuck lived in and shared God's game plan.

A PRAYER YOU CAN PRAY

Father God, I beg You to help me approach You the way You desire. Change how I see you, how I relate to You, and how I seek Your plan for my life. Change how I see and approach the Bible so I'm excited to hear You specifically speaking to me. Empower me with Your Holy Spirit to understand and live out Your game plan in every moment of life.

ASK MYSELF

- "Am I missing supernatural guidance and wisdom from Father God? How would every aspect of my life change if I was hearing from God on His best vision, perspective, and plans for my life?"

MY ACTIONS

Sometimes I, Jeff, can be clueless or just dumb, but at least I realize this set of actions is a mega-dose. It will take some time, maybe a couple months. That's fine. Pace it. But do read each three times so you can digest it fully.

- I will push the RESET button on my approach to the Bible. I will ask my Father to give me an effective approach to the Bible as His day-to-day message to me. I will be intentional. I will carve out time. I will listen to a Bible app. I will come to His Word as a son expecting my Father to show and speak good things to me. I will keep track of what I ask and what He shows me.
- Wherever I am on the journey, I will ask Father God to give me a comprehensive understanding of how this story of humanity began, got off track and is being restored by Jesus. I will ask Him what He wants to show me in each passage I read or listen to.

- I will read these passages three times each, in sequence and overlapping, to soak in the story and see how they tie to the others:
  — Genesis chapters 1-3
  — John 1 & 3
  — Romans 1 & 5
  — Colossians 1 about Jesus
  — John 14 & 15 as Jesus speaks about His Father, Spirit, Himself and how to live
  — Acts 1 & 2 about how Jesus' mission and family of followers grew.
  — Revelation 21 & 22 give glimpses and a vision for the future.
- I will use an easy-to-read study Bible and ask God to show me how to internalize it. I will underline, highlight, or bullet point in the margins.
- I will download the *You Version* Bible app and listen in the car or jump into the Bible at various times of the day when I can read or listen to a verse, passage, story, or devotion. I will copy passages that impact me and text them to myself and a friend.

"Go after wisdom and wisdom is a person and that person's name is Jesus. Go after wisdom because that will allow you to make the right decisions for your kids, for your family, for everything you do."

—Paul Cole

LIFT

17

KILL THE CONSUMER— BE AN INVESTOR

Why do so many relationships start with excitement, energy, and high hopes but eventually unravel?

Let's look in an obvious place—football!

Put yourself in the place of an NFL quarterback when an elite receiver joins the team. In the offseason, your workouts together build a rapport and push each other to excel. You get excited for the regular season and dream of the playoffs.

The season starts and you win a few early games. You're passing accurately, making it easy for the receiver to catch. You protect him by keeping your passes in tight windows where defenders are less of a threat. You're keeping your composure in the pocket, not flinching at the blitz. The receiver runs full speed every play, whether he is the targeted receiver, decoy, or blocker.

Your standards for yourself are high and you're putting a lot into helping your teammate succeed. You're trying to make his job as easy as possible. Passes arrive in perfect timing to an accuracy target of one foot. You're investing in his success and the success of the team. You're focused on giving your best. Every play.

Then the games get harder. You notice your receiver's slip-ups, bad routes, and missed catches. You're not playing your best either. Even so, you still manage to eke out a couple more wins.

Then a tough opponent hands you your first loss. You lose the next game, too. Now you're being tested. Your teammate runs a couple of poor routes, doesn't dive for a tough catch and drops a pass. You're miffed but don't say anything to him—yet.

Consider what's going on under the helmet. What are you, the frustrated quarterback, thinking right about now?

You've been bombarded all your life with enticements to self. Advertisements. Messages. It's all about you and what makes you happy and satisfied. *Once you buy this, get those or accomplish that, you've got it made. And, by the way, you deserve it.*

Plus, your talent has opened the way for more me-firsts. *You're the best, a cut above, the envy of men and the desire of women. If you want it, get it.*

That's how the world wants a talented guy like you to think. What you've heard from parents, coaches, and teammates is in the mix too. These thoughts aren't helping you face a few tough losses and a season—and maybe even a career—that's trending downward.

You're one frustrated quarterback. Your receiver isn't trying as hard as he should, and he's not the only one. The offensive linemen aren't protecting you and the play-calling is unimaginative. Why work so hard to throw accurate passes when you're going to get blasted for staying so focused on your receiver? So, you start to protect yourself a bit, throwing to a general vicinity instead of that one-foot target.

Fewer completions. Fewer first downs. Fewer scores. Attitudes sour. Complaints rise. Wins slip away. Losses mount.

The *consumer mindset* creeps in. If this is the way it's going to go, it's best to just ride it out for as long as it takes until you can find a better deal on a team that appreciates your talent. After all, you deserve it.

Or you could go in a different direction. Instead of being the consumer, you could be the investor. Instead of making it all about you, you could make it about others. You could start working hard again and set the example for your teammates. You could replace the blaming and complaining with humility and encouragement.

> Being an investor, instead of a consumer, means replacing blaming and complaining with humility and encouragement.

CONSUMER V. INVESTOR

Consumers expect a lot from others and little from themselves. They look only for personal advantage. They spend and lose valuable capital trying to fulfill their every imagined need. They're short-term.

Investors are long-term. They don't spend on themselves. They bring value to others.

> Investors are long-term, bringing value to others.

As kids, many of us just slide into the pattern of consuming, spending our money almost before it hits the bottom of our pocket. We focus on what we want immediately. The constant allure of ads fuels our desires for instant gratification, and we spend. And spend.

Then, there are those kids who save their money. They think long term, and maybe even with a touch of entrepreneurship. They look for ways to make life better for themselves and others.

Most of us grow up and understand the importance of investing—with its powerful compound returns and equity growth. We see how investors get ahead.

Even so, America is still dominated by consuming. We want new things we never had and new things to replace the uncool, outdated things—that were in style just last month. Advertisers are powerful. There is a cloud of social media and digital marketers who have found their way into every nook and cranny of our attention.

Five thousand ads a day (I'm guessing it's double that for screen-gazing teens) convince us the universe revolves around us and our needs. We're trained to be discontent, yet to think that the next purchase, acquisition, or entertainment experience will deliver those elusive feelings of satisfaction.

> Consumers believe the universe revolves around them. Investors prioritize dedicated relationships.

More importantly, we remain consumers in our relationships, which have far more impact on the quality of our life than finances. How positive and powerful would the impact be if we became astute and dedicated relationship investors? What if we prioritized investing in our relationship with God, our wife, family, friends, and those we care for and lead?

CONSUMERISM IN RELATIONSHIPS

A few years ago, I asked a young man, Jeremy Vallerand, what marriage was like for his generation. He was just getting married and was clearly putting some thought into it.

"My generation grew up in a country that has known incredible prosperity and freedom, and we have been inundated with advertisements since we were born. We are the customers, and the customers are always right. We have been taught not to be satisfied with what we have. We need to update and upgrade constantly, or we become outdated and irrelevant. Most of us have never had to learn how to be content.

> The mindset of marriage is at odds with the mindset of consumerism. Consumerism teaches me not to be satisfied and look elsewhere. Marriage is a commitment to build satisfaction by investing.

If you've never learned how to stay committed to something despite how it feels, it will be that much harder to succeed in marriage. The mindset of marriage is at odds with the mindset of consumerism. Unless we make a blatant effort to view our spouse differently than we have been taught to view everything else, we will slip back into our consumer-focused behavior without even knowing it.

We have to realize that marriage isn't about getting and taking; it's about giving and exchanging. It's not anchored in what you feel; it's anchored in what you believe and whom you are committed to. It's not self-focused, it's self-sacrificing. By doing this, we can really improve the chances of successful marriages for Generation Y."

I bet most of us from generations before and after Jeremy's can admit to thinking the same way—and we must take the same measures to fix it.

FOCUSING ON OTHERS

NFL coach and broadcaster Tony Dungy once told me, "The biggest thing I've learned in my career and life is that when I focused on myself in life, in a job, or on a team, it didn't work out well. But when I really tried to help other people, it really worked out well."

> "When I focused on myself in life, in a job, or on a team, it didn't work out well. But when I really tried to help other people, it really worked out well."
> —Tony Dungy

Mark Merrill and Tony Dungy are close friends and partners in the organization All Pro Dad, which helps fathers engage with their children. I've known Mark for decades—he definitely has an investor mindset.

Mark joked with me that because he's an attorney, he had to do research to learn how to be a good husband and parent. "So, I dug into the blueprints by studying the Bible. I started trying to do it. I've tried hard, and done decently at times, but I really fall short."

"I discovered I can't do this stuff on my own strength and character. I need God to do it. It's not me; it's Christ loving through me. In 1st John, it says that love comes from God, and we must know God to *know* His love so we can *do* love. I have no possibility of loving my wife and kids as God intended without Christ living in me, by his Holy Spirit's presence. My human strength is not enough. It only works if I'm a vessel for God

> Receiving God's love equips me to love others.

to love people through me. I have to empty my ego, selfish desires, and control to seek to be filled by the Holy Spirit. When my ego and will become less, God does more."

Mark is describing the keys to manhood. He discovered that he needs to live as a son of his Father God. He needs to receive God's love to be able to love others. Mark has transformed over the years from a smart lawyer who tried hard, to a humble son who lets God invest in others through him.

OUT-BLESSING OTHERS

Several years back, when I was leading the organization Stronger Families, I was challenged by a one-line life tip given to me by a wise friend. I needed to improve as an executive leader and was fortunate enough to be coached by Dr. Scott Sticksel. He floated a radical principle in my direction that, at first, I struggled to receive. But as I've tried to put it into practice over the years—imperfectly, I admit—I've found it to be empowering and liberating. Here it is:

> There is great freedom and joy in aiming to out-bless others.

Always aim to out-bless other people.

I initially struggled with this thought. As a competitive, mission-minded guy, I was always looking to recruit people to our cause. Who could I meet? How could I convince them to join our mission? I was raising funds, searching for board members, and trying to expand our network.

I was looking for investors, but I wasn't always investing in them.

I've since learned there is great freedom, mutual benefit, and joy in aiming to out-bless people. The very best relationships are not transactional

> The very best relationships are not transactional or conditional, but about planting seeds of love and concern.

or conditional, but about planting seeds of love and concern. If there are any requests to be made of one another, the timing and results are completely up to God.

I'm learning to stop assessing how others will bless me. It's far better to concentrate on blessing them, encouraging them, serving them, and letting expectations go.

YOUR TURN

You wouldn't be reading this book if you didn't want to add value to the lives of those you love. But let's face it: we are conditioned to think, behave, and react like consumers. We're trying to feel good by feeling good about ourselves, by getting what our gut tells us to get—approval, applause, comfort, pleasure, prosperity, and success.

> Consumer conditioning poisons our view of women, marriage and parenting. It shrinks men.

This is poisoning our relationships. Too often, we look at women through the lenses of satisfying our desires for sexual enjoyment and personal approval. Many guys are connecting, hooking-up, dating, marrying (or holding off marrying) because they're takers and users rather than men who love and commit, honor and serve.

This same consumer approach pollutes our approach to parenting. We want our kids to look good, make the team, earn first place, connect with the right group, get into the best (i.e., most impressive) school, excel, excel, excel. Thriving and excellence are great, but deep down, a lot of it is to impress and make *us* feel good about *ourselves*.

That's selfishness and small-minded consumerism. Impressing others (or even ourselves) has diseased our culture and, in many cases, our churches.

Jesus is the opposite. He invested *everything* to rescue us. He was the most humble, courageous, and sacrificial investor. He tells us to relate to all people with His same humble focus on them. Jesus wants us to receive our new identity as investors in exchange for our old identity as consumers. He invites us to reject the self-defeating corrosion of pride and selfishness so that He can empower us to live for others as He did.

That's the blueprint for manhood. That's God's design for masculinity.

> The blueprint for manhood includes receiving my new identity as an investor in exchange for my old identity as a consumer.

JESUS, THE ULTIMATE INVESTOR

Jesus made the effort and sacrifice to always do the best for others. He is the ultimate investor, and He gives us His empowering presence to live and invest the way He calls us to. Let's look at a few of the ways Jesus invested:

- He invested time in His relationship with His Father in knowing Scriptures and in getting alone for solitude and prayer. He humbly chose to be publicly baptized by His cousin John and courageously chose to face the most intense temptation during 40 days in the wilderness.
- He invested Himself in the lives of scores of forgotten, rejected, sick, disabled, demon-oppressed, and sin-damaged people. He gave them time, attention, dignity, forgiveness, healing, hope, and release from sin.
- He invested His reputation by intervening on behalf of a humiliated woman caught in adultery, standing between her and a vicious mob that was intent on stoning her. He forgave her and rewrote her future.

- He invested by sacrificing His comfort to walk into a raging storm to rescue His disciples.

- He invested His presence and empathy with Martha and Mary as they grieved the death of their brother Lazarus. He also turbo-charged their faith by bringing Lazarus back to life, proving He was the life-giving God Himself.

- He invested patience and perseverance in turning His rough-around-the-edges disciples into deep friends and preparing them to carry on His mission after His departure.

- He invested in Peter by forgiving his huge failure of denying Jesus. He validated his future spiritual leadership with *Gideon Principle* affirmation and vision.

- He invested in many meals with His friends and created celebrations of remembrance. At His farewell feast, He humbly inverted roles and knelt to wash His disciples' dirty feet. Then He broke bread and shared His cup of wine to show them how to remember His sacrificial death and transcending love.

- He invested in His Father's will instead of His own. In the garden He took His pain to His Father. He prayed "not My will, but Yours" so He could choose to pay for our just punishment. He endured horrific crucifixion to rescue those who believe and receive Him.

The Bible coaches us to have the same humble attitude, mindset and approach to relationships that Jesus had. The examples above show his humility, love and patience. He was intentional, committed and courageous in His sacrifice. The results? He brought out the best in His disciples, friends, and all those He helped. He created the best possible relationships for them with Himself, His Father, and one another.

> Jesus is my model for investing—for the Father, in others, and in the most important issues of life.

Jesus deferred the immediate gratification and glory to invest in the very best and glorious future.

Do you want excellent relationships? The consumer approach won't fly. God shows us the way and calls us to be relationship investors. I paraphrase His message in the apostle Paul's letter to Jesus' followers in Philippi, Greece this way:

> Don't do anything out of pride or selfishness, But in humility, consider other people more important than yourself. And don't just look out for your own interest; but look out for the interest of others. In your relationships with one another, have the same humble attitude and self-sacrificing approach of Jesus who invested himself for the very best long-term and eternal outcome for us. (Based on Philippians 2:3-5)

THE CORNBREAD APOLOGY

A few years ago, our extended family rented a beach house for vacation. As I was heading out to the beach one afternoon, my son asked me to get back in time so we could get to a restaurant by 6:15 to accommodate his toddler's bedtime schedule. But I didn't come back until 6:20, showered quickly and acted oblivious to the delay I'd caused. If I said anything at all, it was just "sorry about that," as if it was no big deal (a fairly typical male apology).

That was just Act 1 of *Consumer Jeff* for the evening. Act 2 took place at the restaurant.

The restaurant was known for bringing out its honey cornbread appetizer. Before my son could stop me or distract his son's attention from the cornbread, I grabbed a square and started wolfing it down. My son quickly intercepted the bread board and hid it behind the condiments on the opposite end of the table. He let me know that he wanted us to skip the cornbread for now until our grandson's meal was delivered so he could focus on his entree.

Despite my son's request, I waited for my grandson to look away and snatched another piece. Rolling my shoulder to block his line of sight, I bent down and away and wolfed down my second piece.

This did not go unnoticed by my son. Later in that trip, he said to Stacy, "Mom, I don't get Dad. He's all into 'being an investor' and spending an hour or two in his morning Bible and prayer stuff, but he's still in his own little world where it's all about him."

When Stacy told me what he'd said, I felt a dagger plunge into my gut. It's still painful to remember. I had put my desires ahead of my son's simple request. I had offended him and dented my credibility with one of the most important people in my world.

I *wanted* to be different. I *wanted* to mature. I *wanted* to change. But I needed to act on it. I needed to straight up apologize to my son. I told myself I'd do it.

A couple days later I was at lunch for my weekly huddle with my buddy Greg. I shared that I was considering talking to my son about something in his life that was concerning. Greg simply asked what my credibility was like with my son (anything standing between me and my son to prevent him from hearing my message?). Guess what popped into my mind?

My late-to-dinner and cornbread-wolfing selfishness on our vacation.

After admitting my credibility gap to Greg, I decided to call and apologize. But—I allowed myself to get distracted and waited an entire week (the consumer in me choosing comfort over what was right).

I was driving to the mountain bike trails, and suddenly decided to call right then. I quickly prayed for God to give me the humble tone and clear words. I called my son. I apologized for blowing off his requests that day on our vacation. He was so quick to forgive me. I was amazed, grateful and humbled.

The power of humility and apology is incredible.

It finally hit me that if I wanted to change, there had to be more. I went on and said, "I'm seriously looking at my patterns of *personal convenience selfishness* (I call it PCS) and want to change." I shared with him my realization of the many ways in life I'd been selfish for personal convenience. It helped me to tell my son what I was learning about myself, to ask for forgiveness, and let him know I wanted to change and be accountable. I could sense his appreciation and respect kick in. We felt more comfortable and connected than we had in a long time.

> **My pattern of personal-convenience-selfishness needs to be replaced by considering others first.**

KILL THE CONSUMER. BE AN INVESTOR.

Making changes to be a relationship-investor will take huge doses of self-awareness. You'll ask for and receive some objective feedback as you actively replace selfishness with consideration. And without a doubt, you will make some humbling apologies.

It's all worth it, brothers. I encourage you to receive and take on Jesus' investor mindset. You can begin by asking yourself three key questions:

ASK MYSELF

- "Am I considering the long-term interests of others, or am I focused on my own immediate desires?"
- "Am I about the team or about myself?"
- "What am I giving to this relationship to make it better?"

MY ACTIONS

- I will write a couple of self-coaching notes and post them on my bathroom mirror, phone, or car interior. (Examples: *Am I investing or consuming? Add value, don't drain value. Learn what she needs. Be a relationship investor, dummy!* (Maybe skip that last word, bad self-talk!)
- The best of intentions and goals don't change my life. Habits do. I will show courage and discipline to say NO to time killers and compromises. I will say YES to small, consistent actions that become HABITS. I will choose one or two things to QUIT doing so I have bandwidth to START doing what's best.

"The opposite of love isn't hate; it's selfishness."
—**Mark Merrill**

Love desires and does what is best for another at a cost to self.

18

RELATIONSHIP INVESTING

L ast chapter, we looked at the night and day contrast between being a consumer (our human and societal default) and an investor (The Way of Jesus). Let's see how it plays out in the paramount relationships of marriage and fatherhood, where joy or misery hinge on whether we're a relationship investor or consumer.

THE INVESTOR HUSBAND

When I married, I was a twenty-four-year-old quarterback, hungry to get faster, stronger, and sharper. Committed to improving, I welcomed coaching. Sadly, that didn't carry over into every area of my life.

When it came to my marriage, I figured I was fine. I married a beautiful, virtuous, and strong woman who looked young and behaved maturely. I entered the most important relationship in life unaware. I was

Be a Relationship Investor

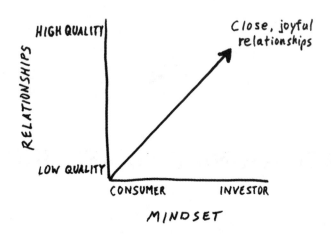

thinking, *She's wonderful. I'm a good guy and I love her like crazy. Marriage will be easy. It's gonna be fun—all the time.* I was naïve, self-focused, and had more pride than self-awareness or desire to mature.

We both paid a price for my lazy approach. Even though we had a divorce-is-not-an-option commitment, there was too much friction and not enough fun.

We were two dominant leader-type personalities, different in almost every other personality trait. But I didn't think I needed to change. I thought our problems were her fault. I assumed she should want what I wanted. I didn't see my faults or acknowledge when I hurt her feelings. (I've been learning that I hate the pain of feeling like a failure when I wound her.) I either laughed things off, sarcastically defended myself, or turned the table to criticize her tone in telling me how I'd disappointed her. On more than one occasion, I justified my actions: "I'm way better than my dad."

I graded myself on a curve. When Stacy expressed hurt or disappointment with how I treated her, I quickly assessed that I'd handled it better than Dad would have, and I told her so.

You can imagine how much that helped.

I was slow to wake up to the realities of my flaws and lack of empathy. Fortunately, our desire for a better marriage pulled us to seek help through mentors and marriage conferences.

Please don't put off getting help like I did. There's hope, freedom and progress ahead of you. There's growing lifelong companionship with a woman who respects and loves you. Let God initiate your transformation. Quit coasting as a consumer. Invest

> Quit coasting as a consumer. I want to invest by listening, learning, and improving.

by listening, learning, and continually improving. Single, divorced, or married—hurt or frustrated, start today.

WHAT'S THE WINNING PLAY?

Late in my rookie season with the Rams, the coaches sent me into my first game. I was not well prepared. Losing badly in the fourth quarter, backed up on our own five-yard line. I was about to throw my first pass in the NFL. I dropped back into the end zone, felt the surge of the defensive line, barely glanced downfield, and launched a bomb—which was caught—by the wrong team.

Five years later, I was traded to the San Francisco 49ers to back up the legendary Joe Montana. When Joe got injured in our first game, I was ready. Coaches Bill Walsh and Mike Holmgren had prepared me to execute our most effective play action pass: *Brown Right, Fox 2, Z Post*. Jerry Rice scored 6 TDs on that play alone during the six games I played, before Joe returned.

Brilliant playbook and game plan. Superb coaching. Intelligent play-calling. Wouldn't it be great if we had those same features in place for our marriages?

God has done that for us. He gave us the game plan in the Bible. Guidance by His Spirit (coaching and strength). Have I mastered His game plan? No. Am I learning? Yes, sometimes the hard way.

I have a bad habit of interrupting Stacy. One day, I did it way too much. Instead of apologizing, I made myself the victim, avoiding my feelings of failure and devaluing hers. I let two days of cold isolation grow between us. Thankfully, my huddle call with deep friends helped me get back to God's game plan. Processing it with them helped me understand her feelings, how I frustrate her, and then hurt her. I apologized. Stacy and I returned to being a team of one.

Let's look at a core of God's marriage game plan for husbands—from 1 Peter 3:7 NLT & AMP:

- In the same way *(that Jesus submitted to His Father's will and sacrificed to love us)*, you husbands, honor, value, and prioritize your wife's concerns.
- Treat your wife with understanding as you live together *(with gentleness, tact, and intelligent regard for her nature, needs and the marriage's health)*.
- She may be physically weaker than you are, but she is your equal partner in God's gift of new life.
- Show her honor and respect so your prayers will not be hindered or ineffective.

Here's more from the book of Ephesians:

"Live together with all humility and gentleness, with patience, bearing with one another in love, eager to maintain the unity of the Spirit in the bond of peace." (Ephesians 4:2-3 ESV).

I encourage you to dig into the whole book of Ephesians. The first three chapters describe our relationship with God and the second three chapters give reliable and counter-cultural wisdom for our relationships with people.

Let's look at this passage phrase-by-phrase and receive some sound coaching for husbands.

1. *Live together*—Weave your time, interests, money, and activities together. Don't just co-exist. Date her, pay attention to her, listen closely, coordinate schedules, share responsibilities.

2. *with all humility*—Humility is the key to appreciation, consideration, service, and the ability to apologize and forgive. Pride is anti-relational. It compares, competes and divides. Remember, Jesus is not just the model of humility; He's the source of it. We receive it when we get serious about making Him the center of our life.

3. *and gentleness*—Relationships require trust. For your wife to trust and open up to you, she needs to feel safe in your care. Gentleness calms her, draws her near, and even helps her to forgive you. Gentleness defuses anger. Watch your words and tone and ground them in love.

4. *with patience*—An investor is willing to wait, but a consumer demands it now. A consumer husband thinks, *me first*; an investor husband thinks, *my wife first*.

> Jesus is not just the model of humility; He's the source of it.

5. *bearing with one another in love*—Loving an imperfect and very different person in a broken world requires hanging in there, some suffering, and always persevering. You prove your love when she's not so lovable. Seek to understand her. Give up complaining and criticizing.

6. ***eager to maintain the unity of the Spirit***—God's Spirit bonds us together. Oneness in marriage comes from a triple braid of husband, wife, and God's Spirit. To get close to your wife, get close to God. Remember, she's your teammate, never your enemy. The enemy is the devil.

7. ***in the bond of peace***—Take responsibility for the health of your marriage. Lead by being the peacemaker. Bond with her by praying with her briefly every day. Be first to apologize, and quick to forgive.

So, Jeff, you're telling me to be perfect. That's not realistic and it's incredibly frustrating.

I agree. You and I cannot drum up enough love, empathy, and kindness. That is God's work. Only He can enable us to love and live this way and, even then, we will sometimes fail. But God has given us a way to persevere. It's receiving. It's humility. It's teamwork. It looks very much like a weekly huddle of Level 5 Friends discussing and praying about their relationships and husbanding.

When we see ourselves accurately, admit our dependence on God, and ask for His help, we can recover and continue. Authentically real. Intent to benefit others. Good men aren't afraid to admit when they're wrong. They don't withhold apologies. They grow and improve.

Love is not finite, in marriage or in life. There is no limit on kindness, encouragement, affirmation, empathy, validation, or grace. Though a good marriage requires energy, intentionality, and patience, don't forget that it takes much apologizing and forgiving. But these hard things add happiness. We don't lose by humbling ourselves. We don't lose by getting rid of defensiveness. We don't lose by sacrificing. Kindness and generosity bring enrichment.

But Jeff, I don't have enough patience, energy, and generosity to consistently invest like this.

Me either. The whole point of being a real and good man is that we don't perform it. We receive it. We receive the guiding power to be a loving husband from our Father God and Jesus.

A husband's love is much more than a feeling. Four decades in, I have to admit this is my challenge. I feel my feelings better than hers! Love is "studying" your wife and praying for God's insight so that you can relate to her with understanding, empathy, and sensitivity to her unique personality,

> My being a real and good man is not an issue of performance, but reception— receiving the guiding power from the Lord.

backstory, needs, and dreams. Cooperate with God to bring out the best version of her by humbly guiding her to Father God to meet her deepest needs. Support her joy and growth.

Be responsible. You're meant to be the human representation of the rescuing, loving, and healing Jesus. Play your role to nurture the heart and soul of the wife God gave you.

PRACTICAL STRATEGIES

My friend Mike gives himself a daily reminder to invest in his wife. Each morning, he looks in his bathroom mirror and sees a sticky note he posted there that says, *"Would I want to be married to me?"* He's coaching himself to focus on his wife by delivering his love to her.

Write down, internalize and talk with friends about these **three investor husband strategies**:

Love by choosing—Prioritize her. Receive every aspect of your wife each day as God's gift to you. Frequently tell and show her (so she feels it) that you cherish her above other things in life.

Lead by serving—Initiate and take responsibility for your relationship, your wife's emotional safety and the quick resolution of conflicts. Set the positive tone in your home. Pray with her each day. Meet her needs. Help her thrive.

> Present or future investor husband strategies: (1) love by choosing; (2) love by serving; (3) love by exclusivity.

Loyalty by exclusivity—Be unconditionally committed to her. Focus all your sexual and romantic interests exclusively on your wife. No comparisons, no porn, no wandering eyes, no fantasizing, no other women.

THE INVESTOR DAD

There's no greater calling than fatherhood. But, if we're honest, most of us don't know how to do it well. Besides the new emotions, questions and responsibilities, many men come into fatherhood with the shortcomings of their dad's example.

Please hear this: You won't understand how to be a dad on your own. The software is not pre-loaded. Like your identity, you *receive* it. Ask Father God to guide you and find seasoned dads or grandads as mentors. Fatherhood is a team effort.

> Fathering can't be outsourced. I must point my children to the Heavenly Father from whom we get our direction.

Dads, we need to seek and receive God's goal of fathering our children the way He loves, trains, and disciplines us. He invites us to connect with Him to receive His wisdom, grace, and strength to father our kids in His way.

We can't outsource fathering to mom, coaches, church groups, or the school of hard knocks. If we don't get help from God and other quality dads, we're going to leave our kids empty, frustrated, confused, and angry.

I started to get God's game plan for fathering at *Pro Athletes Outreach* conferences that Stacy and I attended. I found out that my job was to point my children to our loving heavenly Father and the ways of Jesus. My kids belong to God, not Stacy and me. My job was to steward them with love, protection, and guidance. That means train, discipline, equip, encourage, and pray—with them and for them.

It is a journey, full of humility, learning, engagement and plenty of apologizing. Take a long-term mindset like an investor and rely on God's grace. Good fathering is a team effort. Seek some coaching and a mentor. Process what's going on with your huddle buddies.

THE JOURNEY OF FATHERHOOD

Convince your kids they are loved and valuable. Their emotions get thrashed by society's conditional valuation of who they are and its obsession with appearance, performance and popularity. They're growing up in a brutal social media-saturated world of bullying and capricious comparison. Dads need to show them what is unconditional: God's love and our love. They need your arm around their shoulder and your affirming voice during their most insecure moments and seasons.

But you won't convince them of anything without a positive relationship. Relationship provides the credibility and context for everything else. They need to know you're truly interested and enjoy them for who they are, not who you want them to be. So, be interested—and show it. Ask questions about what they like and about their friends. Affirm your love with hugs, kisses, fist bumps and special handshakes. Be specific with praise and flood them with encouragement.

That confidence will go a long way. But, like we've seen in earlier chapters, they need to receive their identity and love from God. Your job is to ensure your child knows he or she is God's valuable masterpiece.

Dads, the ultimate goal is for their relationship with Jesus to become real. Then, their conscience works, and they will listen to and hear Father God direct them in life.

This means we give up control and avoid pampering or doing the hard stuff for them. We're far more effective when we model God's grace. We can encourage them to try out responsibility and make mistakes while they're under our roof. Those mistakes are less costly than after they've headed out of the house.

Dads need to protect and equip their daughters to insist on excellent character in a boyfriend and husband. Dads train sons to honor and protect women and to choose excellent character in a girlfriend or a wife. Modeling, discussing and training in healthy relationships and the vision for marriage will shape their life. This crucial responsibility and opportunity is yours. Go get help and lean into it.

Your role as dad will change throughout your child's life. Early on, you're a provider and protector. Then a play pal, leader, teacher, and spiritual guide. Eventually, you do more training and coaching. In their midteens, your role turns to consultant and encourager. When they launch as adults, your big challenge is to give them the respect and space you desired as a young man. It's crucial, though not easy, to press STOP on the unsolicited advice.

GIVING GOD'S BLESSING

Dads, we only get two fast decades to live out our most essential roles of modeling faith and discipling our children in the life-giving ways of Jesus. In many ways, God's blessing is the epitome of everything we've been talking about.

When Jesus was thirty years old, He asked His cousin John the Baptist to baptize Him. His Father spoke words of blessing over Him, "This My beloved Son, in whom I am well-pleased and delighted." (Matthew 3:17 AMP)

The blessing is a life-changing gift of unconditional love and affirmation passed down from one generation to the next. It's a key way to show our children just how highly valued they are.

If you think you've missed the season to bless your child, it's not too late. Though my dad was incredibly affirming throughout my teens and early twenties, I asked him to pray his blessing over me just a few days before he died of cancer at 73.

Lying on his bed, his breath and voice weakened, Dad put his hand on my arm and prayed, *"Dear God, please help Jeff remember his strength and talent [are from God]. Help Jeff remember the force for good he is in the world. And help us both remember—the only thing that matters is 'Thy will be done.'"*

> A good dad is approachable, engaged, and purposeful. And this means I accept God's forgiveness when I blow it.

Those were the last words Dad spoke to me. He called out my strength of identity in Christ. He affirmed my mission to be a force for good. And he took the pressure off me by praying that I'd remember to trust God's goodness and sovereign control. Leave the outcomes up to God.

A good dad aims to be approachable, engaged, and purposeful—just as God is to us when we let Him. If you haven't been that dad, or have some gaps, don't beat yourself up and let shame lead into that victim trap. The past is gone. Accept God's forgiveness, forgive yourself and ask for your children's forgiveness. Then invite their input on what they would like in their relationship with you.

Face your faults. Repent fully. Forgive swiftly. Support the underdog. Celebrate comebacks.

It's never too late to start investing.

ASK MYSELF

- "What improvement and investment would my loved one value most: Loving, Leading, or Loyalty? Does she most need to be Understood, Valued, or Affirmed?"

MY ACTIONS

- *THE RELATIONSHIP CHALLENGE*: At a calm moment, I will ask my wife (or girlfriend), and each of my children: "How can I better love you?"; and "What would you like me to do more, stop doing, or start doing?"
- I will ask her, or my child: "What do you wish I understood about you and our relationship? And I will realize that the greatest investment I can make with my wife or child is a complete apology with a humble request to be forgiven, with zero explanations or excuses. I will do it on a date or when doing something fun like playing a game they enjoy or throwing a football (what else is there to throw!).
- I will use the free relationship counselor Gary Smalley suggested: ask my loved one to rate our relationship on a 1—10 scale. I won't act shocked or debate the number. I will ask what it would take to move it toward a 10. I will work the plan.
- I will pick a special time and place and way to give my child my Blessing (grandchild or someone I mentor). I will look at the Gideon Principle in chapter 5. And I will ask God to help me.

"Not everyone can be famous. But everyone can be great—because everyone can serve."

—Dr. Martin Luther King, Jr.

"Every child, in every home, deserves to have at least ONE person in their life who is CRAZY about them. The Blessing is a biblical tool that can help YOU communicate unconditional love as an unshakable foundation for HEALTH and wholeness—without spoiling or giving false praise to a child that crumbles as they face the challenges and hurts in real life."

—John Trent*

---

* For resources on the Father's Blessing, go to www.strongfamilies.com/parenting

19

BEATING LIFE'S BLITZES

As a quarterback, I actually liked getting blitzed. A blitz meant man-to-man coverage and no deep safety. It was big play time, an opportunity for the deep pass. Sure, blitzes can result in lost yardage. But they can also result in touchdowns. Blitzes are both danger and opportunity combined in one intense situation.

But they're nothing but bad—if you're not prepared.

Life is filled with blitzes. Ever since Adam and Eve rejected God's provision and ignored His boundaries, life on this earth has been messed up. We live under a curse of blindsides and frontal attacks, including difficulty, division, disaster, and death.

But this is not the whole picture. God created and intended a perfect world. He created us as souls who can live with Him beyond the calculated earthly lifespan. He sent His Son as the solution to bring us back to Him. Jesus lived perfectly and died as the one and only sacrifice that could satisfy justice and forgive humanity. Jesus will return to earth again to complete history by judging evil, recreating the earth, and making all things new—for those who receive Him.

The very way that Jesus won victory over death came through the ultimate blitz. His perfect life was cut down in the most brutal way. No one saw it coming, except Jesus. He knew what was coming, and He still signed up for it. He focused on the joy and glory His Father set before Him in heaven.

Beating blitzes is God's paradigm to save us, and it's the archetype for every real and good man. Whether the blitz is caused by disease, addiction, accident, natural disaster, or the sins of others or yourself, God knows about it and has a redemptive strategy for you to face it.

We are made in the image of God and our purpose in life is to become like Jesus (see Romans 8:29). This can change every relationship and situation in our journey as men. The apostle Paul said it directly, "Be conformed to the image of Christ." Our purpose is to become like Jesus so we can pursue God's plan for our life and face blitzes with confidence in Christ's overcoming power.

> Beating blitzes is God's paradigm to save me, but also to transform me and the hard challenges of life into something great.

A real and good man is made to face blitzes and to help others face their blitzes. Once God takes us through a few blitzes, we learn to rely on God's strength to support, comfort, and encourage others (see 2 Corinthians 1:3-4). Here's reality: we don't become like Jesus without facing blitzes. When we allow Him, God uses all these difficulties to mature and transform us. We receive His perspective, His presence, and His approach to life. Our view of Him and of ourselves changes. We find a faith that sticks.

OPPORTUNITY ATTITUDE

When I was 32, I faced a career blitz. My languishing career as a backup quarterback had reignited as I stepped in to quarterback the Seattle Seahawks to three wins and three losses. The sixth of those games was a crucial midseason game on Sunday Night Football. We were playing well and leading the Raiders for three quarters, but we stalled, and they rallied. In overtime, I threw an interception and the Raiders beat us with a field goal on the next play. I was cut after the game.

Facing previous blitzes with God had prepared Stacy and me to handle this one. We knew God was good and was always in charge. We leaned into Him and kept the long term in view.

On Monday afternoon I got a clue from a coach that I'd be cut Tuesday morning. That helped me prepare so I could honor my coaches and teammates and leave them in a positive way. Stacy, our young sons, and my pastor came to my last-minute farewell press conference. I felt God anchoring me and was able to remind my friends in the media and Seattle that I hadn't lost my identity or peace, which were anchored in my relationship with Christ.

A surprise opportunity also came with this blitz. At dinner the night I was cut, our six-year-old prayed, "God, thanks for the food and please give Daddy a new team. I want him to play for the Eagles. Amen." Stacy and I chuckled and wondered where that came from (turns out, he liked eagles and wanted me to have the same team name as his soccer team). But we were blown away early the next morning when the Philadelphia Eagles general manager called to sign me for the rest of the season.

Four weeks later we were in Houston for a Monday Night game. The Oilers pounded us. They knocked our starting QB, Jim McMahon, out of the game. I took over in the third quarter. Their pass rush was brutal, and we had no time for most pass plays. But a dangerous moment offered a sliver of opportunity. On 3rd and 8 from their 20, our coaches called a slow-developing deep pass. Houston blitzed and this was the opportunity we needed. As the ball was snapped, our players quickly scrapped the original play and adapted. I shortened my drop-back to get the ball off before being knocked down by the blitzing free safety. Tight end Keith Jackson canceled his corner route and sped to the goal line on a post route. He caught the pass for our only touchdown and the win.

When we got to the locker room, coach Richie Kotite's Brooklyn accent was thick as he congratulated us and barked out how proud he was of me, while tossing the game ball to me. Recently cut by the Seahawks, barely versed in the Eagles unfamiliar offense, I played a key role and proved myself to my teammates. But it was different from victories in the past. It felt better than pounding my chest and yelling, "I did it!" It felt more pure, like a gift, not a triumph for self. I felt the team's thrill of victory, without the ego. I was grateful and humbled, joyful without the baggage of pride. Gratitude to God flooded me. It was so much better than self-dependence, self–effort, and self-congratulating.

The blitzes you and I face in life don't turn around as fast as a sight adjustment on a Patrick Mahomes' touchdown pass. There are no sudden fixes for the pain and suffering that drag on as you're losing your dad to terminal cancer or going through any of life's deep hardships. It's not natural or easy to bring an opportunity mindset to the pain of childhood traumas that knock you down decades later, or to the collapse in your career and betrayals at work or in marriage. When you're in the dark valley of a family-fracturing divorce, addiction, or the devastating death of a child, it may seem impossible to have God's vision of opportunity. How can we?

MINDSET—LONG-TERM OR SHORT-TERM? ABUNDANCE OR SCARCITY?

Father God assures us it's possible, but only if we first are grateful to rejoice in the greatest victory and treasure He has already given us. Before

I take us to God's coaching on how we rejoice in facing blitzes as opportunity, let's calibrate our perspective with a scenario.

Imagine you just inherited a magnificent and peaceful estate with a 10,000 square foot home, five cars in the garage, guest suites, jacuzzi, pool, waterfalls, and every interior and exterior feature to optimize relaxing, hospitality, and outdoor recreation. You're driving up the half-mile winding driveway for the first time in a rental car. You get a flat tire. Are you agitated and angry—or still excited to see the house? You jump out to inspect the flat and notice that your storage shed for the driving lawn mower is on fire.

How will you handle it? Will you stress out? Become distraught? Will the flat and burned mower's shed stop you from walking up the driveway to live in the home with five new cars in the garage? Or will you still celebrate that you've been given this astounding estate and just suffered a temporary problem and loss? Perspective matters.

The reality of God's love and plans for us are exponentially greater than we realize. Through His Son Jesus Christ, our Father gives us complete forgiveness, peace, and perfect standing with Him. We receive what we could never deserve—unconditional love and adoption into His family. Instead of spiritual death, we get the abundant life of Jesus. His life and the power of depending on His presence in us overcome the heartaches of this broken world. At the end of this winding driveway, He gives us an eternal paradise with Him in His glory.

Knowing that victory is guaranteed, and that Jesus Christ has already won, is revolutionary and life-giving. Here's God's true perspective on trials and coaching for blitzes from Romans 5:1-5 (ESV):

"Therefore, since we have been justified by faith, we have peace with God through our Lord Jesus Christ. Through him we have also obtained access by faith into this grace in which we stand, and we rejoice in hope of the glory of God."

Always celebrate your ultimate victory which Jesus Christ won—
Father God's guaranteed grace, acceptance, peace, and promise of per-
fected eternity in the glory of God.

> *"Not only that, but we rejoice in our sufferings, knowing that suffer-*
> *ing produces perseverance, and perseverance produces character, and*
> *character produces hope, and hope does not put us to shame, because*
> *God's love has been poured into our hearts through the Holy Spirit*
> *who has been given to us."*

Embrace your blitzes, battles, trials, and suffering as opportunities.
Rejoice because God will grow in you persevering faith, character like
Jesus, and hope in a secure eternity. We will receive an overflow of God's
love as we turn to Him in hard times more completely than ever before.

> Manhood received
> from God celebrates
> Christ's ultimate
> victory for me. It sees
> blitzes and battles
> as opportunities to
> grow in grace and
> to honor God.

Men, let's learn to focus on the
opportunity, not the danger. We can
gain transcending gratitude and joy
by focusing on the grand triumph and
eternal treasure God gave us, not the
present loss. Live as a son who depends
on your Father, not yourself. Let's pull
together with our team.

THREE STRATEGIES FOR FACING BLITZES

So how do we face and overcome blitzes?* How do we seize the opportunities?
Not by hunkering down, isolating, or going solo. We depend upon Jesus. We
follow Him. We team up. Here are three strategies from Jesus' example.

---

* You can unpack these strategies more fully in my book, *Facing The Blitz: Three*
Strategies For Turning Trials Into Triumphs.

#1. Keep The Long-Term View

Remember that God is working on a long-term plan for good. Though hard and even evil things happen in this world, God will conclude this era. He will judge evil and reward good. He's drawing us to Him, shaping us, and even using things for good which the enemy schemed for evil. Aim for the eternal goal and keep the big picture in mind.

> I can face and overcome my blitzes by keeping the long-term view, by being humble and willing to change, and by focusing on blessing others.

Focus on truth you'll find in *Genesis 50:20; Romans 8:28; 2 Corinthians 12:9-10; and 2 Thessalonians 3:5.* In the shock of a disappointment, problem, or conflict, pause, pray, and receive your response from God. In the heat of a battle, run to God and your team. Focus on what will turn this for God's best. Cultivate an *opportunity attitude.*

#2. Be Humble and Willing to Change

Seek guidance from God and become self-aware by asking for honest feedback. Share and process your challenge with a couple of trusted friends. Develop Level 5 Friends before or during your blitz. Overcoming requires you to learn. You need to turn away from your own direction and choose the wise and healthy way. Take on the same humility that Christ demonstrated when He came among us as a person, served His flawed friends, and sacrificed Himself for our benefit.

Focus on the truths found in *Romans 8:29; James 5:16; 1 John 1:9; and 2 Corinthians 12:1-2.* Stop doing what hasn't worked. Quit your pride. Ask for help. Stop consuming. Start investing. Embrace the opportunity to persevere by trusting and following Jesus. Consider others before yourself.

Stop avoiding. Stop being deceived by lies and your false narrative. Stop denying, blaming, or lying. Face the truth. Tell the truth. Love in a courageous way. Apologize and forgive. Trust God by getting out of His way instead of trying to control and fix things yourself.

#3. Focus On Blessing Others

You are God's beloved child, and He has blessed you with His love and acceptance. You're not an orphan or victim. By admitting your spiritual poverty, you receive His spiritual and relational riches. He'll make you a relationship investor. Value people and invest in your relationships. When you are attacked and suffering, bless others. Take the Jesus approach.

Focus on the truths found in *John 13:34; 1 Peter 3:9; Proverbs 11:25; and Luke 6:28.* Do what's best for others. Surprise people with kindness and generosity. Restore peace by responding gently. When someone makes your life hard, go the extra mile. Out-bless. When you're the one hurting, look around for someone else who's hurting. Encourage them. Pray for them. Treat people graciously.

Always remember that God is your power source, not yourself. His power flows when you let Him take over. When you belong to Christ and let Him own you, you live with Jesus and His perseverance. You can handle all things "through Him who gives you strength" (Philippians 4:13). But remember, "Apart from Him you can do nothing" (John 15:5, author's paraphrase).

ASK MYSELF

- "Do I have a strategy and team to face life's blitzes as opportunities—or am I just hoping not to be blitzed (because *I don't like blitzes*)?"

MY ACTIONS

- I will review a blitz I faced that led to positive growth. I will create a self-reminder to choose an opportunity-mindset and bullet point my core team and blitz strategy principles.

"In this world you will be blitzed, but have courage not fear, for I have overcome the blitz."
—Jesus as quoted in the NFL translation of John 16:33 (go look it up).

"To reach something good, it is useful to have gone astray."
—St. Teresa of Avila

20

SEX, SECRECY & DIRTY BOMBS

Sex sets up blitzes every man faces. Big blitzes—that carry serious danger—and opportunity.

For the man who loves his wife well, sex can add exhilaration to your marriage and pleasure that fires hormones. These feel-good hormones of dopamine, serotonin, endorphins, and oxytocin can bond you even closer to your wife.

God has never been anti-pleasure. He invented it and put these hormones into your body's chemistry. Your sex drive has a good purpose when it's understood as a gift from God that is channeled by your allegiance to Him and your commitment to one woman.

Attraction is good. But when it crosses over into lust, everything goes haywire. Porn is lust's delivery system. It mutates your expectations of women, sex and pleasure. It rewires your brain—all those hormones are hijacked and used against you to feed an addiction to pleasure, instead of a connection to God and a devotion to your wife.

I don't say this to focus only on porn or shame anyone. It's just one of many addictive consumer experiences our culture feeds us. But let's also not downplay its negative effects.

The cost is high. We lose God's blessing and turn to a counterfeit of love and sex (the devil is a counterfeiter). It sets a timer for a dirty bomb to detonate, blasting and poisoning our lives.

POISONOUS PLEASURE

Sex is mass-marketed in our digital age. It's on our screens 24/7, but it's nothing new—it's been happening for centuries. Entire cultures have suffered for it.

Our society breeds new things to binge on. Women (even youth and children) are presented as objects for consumption. Porn is the most used modern drug. Just like other addictions, today's brains have been rewired to always want more. The damage is piling up. It's getting worse.

Smartphones fill the margins of our time and flood our brains with dopamine-spiking stimulation. Social media builds new on-ramps to porn and hookups. Sexual content spills out constantly, leading, in some cases, to bullying and violence. The pleasure and stress centers in our brains are fired so often that some guys have lost the ability to feel anything at all, including attachment, pleasure, or guilt. Depression and addiction are skyrocketing.

SHAME IS THE DEVIL'S CANCER

If we're going to defuse the bombs, we've got to disarm shame. And that starts by answering some tough questions, like:

- What really controls me?
- What do I turn to when I'm bored, hungry, tired, stressed, discouraged, angry, or ashamed?
- Why do I hide secret parts of my life?

Postmodernism promised that progressive values would rid us of shame. It hasn't panned out. It said happiness would come if we unshackled ourselves from the contrived morals and restrictions associated with God. It hasn't. It doesn't matter that society endorses behavior on the outside if something different happens to us on the inside.

When we do things that feel wrong to us, we experience guilt. Our conscience is God's helpful signal that we're off-track. We can respond by confessing, seeking God's mercy, and receiving His grace to correct our course. We move out of the shadows of secrecy into the light of truth.

Let me warn you: even though guilt *can* call us toward God's kindness, the devil is quick to twist it into unforgiveable shame, making us feel like hopeless failures. Unbiblical shame warps the message of "you *did* a bad thing" (which could help correct us) to "you *are* a bad thing" (which only condemns us). It attacks our identity and worth, which only fuels lies, secrecy, and isolation.

> "Shame eats away at that part of us that believes we're capable of change." —from the movie *Paul's Promise*

It's a cycle. But that kind of shame doesn't have to win.

Please believe that you can beat this blitz—but not alone. Escape the secrecy and embrace a relationship with Father God, the one He wants to have with you.

Let's look at three guys who faced blitzes and turned to God when the bombs exploded.

Reese is young. He faced his blitz during his sophomore year in college. He was rooming with a best friend and wanted to be real with him. Like so many of us, Reese was afraid to talk openly because he struggled with lust and pornography. He felt he should say something about it to his roommate but believed his dark weakness would lose his respect and tank their friendship.

Thankfully, Reese eventually decided to just say the hard thing.

Hey, I struggle with lust. I look at porn.

His buddy didn't close down. In fact, he opened up.

"Opposite of what my fears told me," Reese says, "I felt instant freedom. The weight lifted. We felt closer than before. We both saw the grip of porn and lust loosened."

The next guy was a winsome guy, a young husband. He'd grown up in a close family, was involved in the church, and participated in an accountability group of men that met weekly. He seemed to have it all together.

But he slid into telling half-truths, secrecy, and pretense because of a porn addiction. Getting married to a beautiful girl didn't end it. (Why do we think marriage will fix us?) The porn intensified in the darkness and mushroomed into years of sexual addiction and multiple affairs. He hated it, but, by his own admission, would rather have died than kill his wife's soul by admitting what he'd been doing to her.

But the bomb was more than dirty. It was nuclear and it exploded. He got caught.

The pain was unimaginable, but so was his wife's response. A chorus of caring people suggested divorce. They predicted that he wouldn't be willing to do the work to heal from his sex addiction and become trustworthy. She separated from him—not to punish him, but to heal. This boundary protected her and their kids. It made him face reality and seek comprehensive help.

Exposed and shattered, he turned to a team. He confided in a couple of friends and checked into a recovery center. He embraced honesty and humility. He experienced the real Father God (not the God of his imagination) who radically forgave him.

Fast forward to today: he meets consistently with a recovery sponsor and group. He's also a sponsor, meeting with men who are in the process of recovering. His relationship with God is real, deep and filled with grace. So are his relationships with his friends. After a long separation, his marriage is secure, and his wife is joyful. His family is tight and thriving.

The third guy is older. He had over-the-top success in business, family, philanthropy, and (what seemed to be) faith. A billion-dollar company, private jet, and vacation properties. A lovely wife, a dozen grandchildren. But he'd been hiding a secret: porn and sex addiction. A prostitution sting and arrest surfaced the lies and blew up his life. His business, his reputation, and nearly everything went away . . . except his wife who God reached in a clear and powerful way.

His healing began when he realized the root of it all, his worst trait—lying.

"In my pain, God became more real to me than anything else. He showed me that lying is one of the worst things a believer can do, because lying is what Satan does. Lying aligns us with God's enemy, the 'father of lies.' It makes us lie to ourselves and believe the lies Satan tells us."

He explained that he'd ignored his lying habit for many years. Getting away with it made everything worse. But when he faced his fatal flaw, he was able to trace its roots back to fairly typical habits of making excuses for the bad and exaggerating the good. It's easy to do in life, in projecting an image or in telling a fish story . . . or in hiding porn and betraying his wife. He was covering deceit with a veneer of success, family activity, and Christian philanthropy.

He was mocked in the news. Some abandoned him, but he was blown away by so many true friends who reached out to care for and encourage him. He found total forgiveness from God. He found grace and complete forgiveness from his wife. In her crisis, she encountered the love and guidance of God. She poured her heart out in conversation with God and heard His reply—be Him to her husband, forgive and love him like Jesus. That forgiveness from God and his wife is how God melted and rebuilt him.

After hitting the very bottom, wailing for hours, he felt God warmly envelop Him and authoritatively tell him, "Never lie and I will be by your side." He'd been a functional alcoholic but committed to God and his wife that he would never drink or lie again. He adopted an antidote to lying—always correct yourself on the spot.

> The secrets and damage of sexual addiction plead for me to be real, to address my flaws and vices, to face my past traumas, and to get help.

Once again, God's miraculous grace carried a man and his family through a horrific blitz when they depended fully on Him. A few deep friends loyally walked with him. God restored their marriage and family. Many things, including image, were lost, but not the most important things.

These stories plead with us to be real—quit lying, be honest, address our junk, face our past traumas, get help and let God take over.

Let's get tactical. How does a man defuse the bombs?

> Seven essentials in the healing path: humility, acceptance, confession, responsibility, forgiveness, transformation, and connection.

I shared a meal with Steve Arterburn, founder of *New Life Ministries,* at a *Fatherhood CoMission* summit. Steve has over 40 years of experience dealing with men's deepest problems and addictions (including those traced to childhood abuse and various trauma). I asked him if there was a clear and proven healing path to help men overcome the most serious blitzes he treats. He jotted down these seven essentials. I added the coaching (in italics).

1. Surrender (Humility). *Let God lead and stop faking.*
2. See it (Acceptance). *Face reality and root problems.*
3. Say it (Confession). *To others and to God.*
4. Own it (Responsibility). *Get treatment and support.*
5. Release it (Forgiveness). *Receive God's forgiveness and reject shame.*
6. Reverse it (Transformation). *With God as your priority and focus.*
7. Preserve it (Connection). *With teamwork and discipleship.*

Let the power and the forgiveness of Jesus catalyze your healing.

Do you feel undeserving because of your failings and secrets? Consider how God treated a man who, while married, lusted after an employee's young wife, slept with her, stole her away, and had her husband killed. This man's failures detonated huge bombs. Yet, God called him "a man after My own heart." How could that be?

Because of God's grace, the man loved God deeply and repented totally, sprinting to God after failures and whenever he was under pressure. He knew God was a God of forgiveness (a thousand years before Jesus even arrived to prove it). The man was David, the King of Israel, from whose family would come God's Messiah, Jesus.

Go to Father God like David did—all the way. Let His forgiveness and acceptance give you the courage to disclose your struggles to your closest friends. Get professional help and battle-proven spiritual help. Stop being mad at yourself. Get mad at the source of the lies, the devil. Fill the desires in your heart with the only relationship that satisfies. Let God channel your passions and emotional needs into natural joy and healthy pleasure.

Remember, if you do get bombed, you don't have to be nuked. And once you end the secrecy, you might find that there are fewer ticking bombs. Stay humble and aware of your vulnerabilities. Turn to God and a close team of friends, and you can defuse any of them.

ASK MYSELF

- "What's the root of my risk areas—sexual detours, corrosive habits, and self-medicating substances or activities—a childhood wound, an identity deficit, an abuse or trauma that triggers shame, secrecy, and emotional stuffing? What accepted LIE, inner FEAR or driving EMOTIONAL NEED led me off track or pushed me to self-medicate to cope?"

MY ACTIONS

- To kill lies, shame, and fear, I need to fully receive Jesus' love, forgiveness and acceptance. I will ask God to show Himself to me. I will ask Him where He wants to start changing my life. I will respond to Him.
- I will take the first step, and the next step, into the light. I will tell one safe person who can help me open up to honesty and seek whatever help I need. I will call on my real friends.

A great sex life comes from exclusivity and nurturing a great marriage relationship.

21

MISSION HIMPOSSIBLE

*D*o you want your life to be meaningful?

Do you want a purpose that keeps you motivated, something that will outlive you?

Do you want to be remembered as a man who made a positive impact?

I do. But I don't trust myself to best define that purpose, let alone pursue it in the best way.

What I've said about our identity must also be true of our purpose—it's not something we come up with on our own. We have to *receive* it from the

> I receive both my identity and my purpose from the Father.

Father. As Jesus modeled so faithfully, we need to listen to the Father. When we do, we will receive more than His guidance, He will give us courage and confidence, too. His purpose comes with His power.

The key to receiving this purpose and confidence from God is humility—trusting God's guidance, timing, and His outcomes. It's being grateful, giving Him the glory for everything that unfolds.

You and I are "on mission" at all times. In the moment-to-moment stuff of life, in every interaction with people, and in the long-range opportunities to help transform lives. From an hour at work to an hour working through a conflict with your wife (in a way that leads to her feeling better understood and loved by you). From lifting weights to lifting a friend's hopes and courage. Anything can matter. Nothing is extraneous. Our mission as a man, as God's valued son, is 24/7/365.

We're fooling ourselves if we don't remind ourselves that God alone controls outcomes. His book of beginnings, Genesis, describes God creating all things, including mankind. He made Adam and Eve in His image and likeness. He gave them a noble purpose, to be productive and fruitful and to manage His creation on earth. They could have succeeded in this mission—until they tried to do it their own way. They stepped away from their relationship with God. Paradise in the garden was lost, for them and for us. Separating from God messed up our mission to multiply and bring out the best in God's world. It rendered the life of thriving in peace and innocence impossible. Eternally impossible.

But then God sent the solution. Grace. Jesus stepped into our world and solved our problem of sin-induced separation. Peace was given and purpose regained through Christ. The impossible mission became the Him-possible mission. (Corny spelling, but conceptually accurate.) Our life only becomes what God designed it to be when we make it about Him and by Him.

God wants us to thrive fully as we receive from Him our personalities, strengths, stories, and relationships. We'll excel if we tie into His WHY, His greatest mission—to bring Him glory. Remind yourself daily of the renowned answer to the question of man's chief purpose? *"To glorify God, and to enjoy him forever."* [The Westminster Shorter Catechism]

A college basketball coach said the same in his own way. Tony Bennett, at the University of Virginia, described his life purpose:

> *If my life is just about winning championships, if it's just about being the best, then I'm running the wrong race. That's empty. But if it's about trying to be excellent and do things the right way, to honor the university that hired me, the athletic director I work for and the young men I'm coaching—always in the process trying to bring glory to God—then that's the right thing.*

Our ultimate purpose is to steward life for our Creator. Since sin has damaged humanity and the world, God's mission is to reconcile lost people and a broken world back to Him. He involves us, His sons, and daughters, in His mission. We participate with Jesus in connecting people back to Him (vertically) and improving their lives on earth (horizontally).

> My ultimate purpose is to steward life for my Creator.

Let's tie it together. We are stewards of the life and gifts God has given us. He is our priority, and our goal is to give Him glory. God invites us to join Him in His mission to reconcile people and improve life. We do it by loving God and loving others. That translates into purposes like doing our work with excellence, protecting the vulnerable, uplifting others, and improving situations and lives according to God's wisdom.

REAL MEN HAVE A REAL MISSION

Being on mission with God means that we are ambassadors for Jesus Christ. God's message to us in 2 Corinthians 5:17-21 describes our mission. Reading this passage feels like a son hearing his dad affirm and call him into ownership and leadership of the family's superb business. Here's how I hear it:

When you receive Jesus Christ, the old you is gone. A new you has come because I brought you back as my son. You are accepted and right in my eyes because I have put the righteousness of Christ in you. I love you unconditionally; I have canceled all your sin. Now, as I'm inviting the world to come back into my family, I'm inviting you to join me. I'm giving you a mission, a message, and a title. Your mission is reconciliation. Your message is "God reconciles people. Please return to Him." Your title is Ambassador for Christ. Be with me in this work.

Remember my friend Marvin who was so damaged and lost? (I shared some of his story in chapters 6 and 13.) He used women, damaged many people, and neglected his own children. He was an entrepreneur of the streets. But eventually legal threats and drug rehab triggered a change in him. He was brought to His perfect Father by Jesus Christ and a radical transformation began. Marvin's mission soon became all about reconciling with his family and beginning to build those relationships that he had long neglected. He persevered through the labyrinth of child support enforcement, DHS, and other governmental hurdles to marry Jeanett, the woman he loved who was the mother of his youngest child. He got a job and then gathered his other children into his and Jeanett's family.

As he rebuilt his life, Marvin discovered his strengths and his true passion—his life mission—helping other disconnected dads reconcile with their children. He and Jeanett founded the organization DADS for this purpose.

God changed Marvin from a selfish man into a generous man. He's now an entrepreneur for good, investing his leadership talents to reconcile dads and families. DADS protects, defends, and rescues women, children, and struggling men. Marvin says gaining a compelling mission changed him.

I turned the corner when I saw that I could help other men see God turn their lives around. I realized that life and God's kingdom are bigger than just getting my life right. I'd been part of the problem and here was an opportunity to be part of the solution—using my gift to speak into other men's lives and help them navigate through complex, discouraging systems to reconnect with their kids and reunite their family.

Marvin describes how shifting our focus can help us become better men: *"When you start pouring into others to help them make their lives better, you have truly found the keys to manhood. The feelings I have as I help others enjoy being a father, a family, and a success are more satisfying than my own success. I love to see other men's transformation."*

Like it did in Marvin, the transformation God has done in our lives goes a long way toward shaping our mission and purpose. We don't have to be perfect, but we do need to be honest. Real men are honest men who are being changed by the power of Christ and who are helping others know Christ like they do.*

Jesus modeled how to live on mission. He reconciled people to the Father and constantly used His power to lift people out of hopelessness. He healed, fed, taught, forgave, and transformed them. He protected the outcast. He lifted burdens. He prepared His disciples for servant-based leadership by washing their feet and giving them vision for a new and eternal kingdom characterized by love.

The way of Jesus is compelling. It's the way real good men live when they receive it.

AMBASSADOR IN A GOLF SHIRT

You don't need an extreme story to feel God's pleasure or make an impact. My friend Rich's backstory is nothing like Marvin's, but his mission is just as profound.

---

* Marvin and Jeanett and the board, staff and volunteers of DADS have mentored over 4,000 dads, reconciling thousands of families and children to experience the security and love of a present and engaged dad. DADS stops cycles of fatherlessness. www.AboutDads.org

Rich is a partner in a financial planning firm, and I'll say this: he stewards relationships as well as he does investments.

Rich likes to golf, and he likes to encourage other men, so he participates in an annual golf trip with work colleagues and other guys in the investment business. One year, he and Tony, a man from another firm, arrived early so they went to dinner together. When they finished eating, Tony asked Rich, *"Want to go to a strip club?"*

Rich kept his response low key. With no show of disapproval or criticism he declined with a simple, *"No, I really don't."*

Tony was surprised. *"Why not?"*

"Well," Rich replied, *"I'm married. If I go to a strip club, I'm just gonna get my engine riled up and there's nothing I could do because my wife isn't here with me. So, I just think it would be kind of dumb. And I'm a Christian. I love God and He really loves people. He loves women. He loves marriage and He loves sexual enjoyment in marriage. I don't feel it's a healthy or smart thing to do because I'm committed to God."*

A year later Rich and Tony drove together to the golf resort. Tony piped up, *"Hey Rich, guess what happened to me?"* He slaps Rich's leg and blurts out, *"I'm one of you now!"*

"What?"

"I'm one of you now. I became a Christian. And it's all because you wouldn't go to a strip club!"

"What do you mean?"

"When you said no to going to the strip club and talked about your wife and God and what was best, it made me scratch my head. I started thinking about how I don't have any knowledge of God and why my marriages have been so messed up. So, I went on a journey. I tried to figure out who God was, and I found Jesus Christ."

That's Rich, an ambassador for Christ, working in finance, enjoying golf, and having dinner with a buddy. No pulpit or soapbox. Just clarity about who loves him, who he loves, and how he lives.

A man representing Jesus stewards opportunities like this for God's purposes. Opportunities like talking with a colleague or client, coaching a little league team, or volunteering at a food pantry. It's you asking a work buddy about his life or sharing the awesome reality that Jesus forgives and sets us free to walk on a better path.

Wherever you are, whatever you do—an ambassador for Christ—that's you.

ASK MYSELF

- "What's my purpose in life and how did I determine it?"
- "Who does it serve and who powers it—me or God?"

MY ACTIONS

- I will determine my single greatest strength, my driving passion, who I most want to help and the sweet spot when I'm working at my best and feeling the most joy and satisfaction. I will bullet point those in strong language that speaks to me.
- I will draft a phrase for my life purpose and a sentence for my mission statement. I will go to God to determine and empower it. I will ask how it can link God's glory, His reconciling mission, and employing my greatest strengths and gifts to love others and improve lives.

"I am the vine; you are the branches. Those who live in surrendered connection with Me, and I live in them, will produce much fruit. For apart from Me you can do nothing."
—Jesus in John 15:5 NLT

22

THE BEST OWNER

Steve wanted to spend a day together to discuss his legacy—the future of his family and a dilemma weighing him down over the future of his business (he owns a large cause-advancing marketing firm). For decades he had poured himself into his career helping Christian organizations succeed in their ministry goals; he wanted to finish well. But he was deeply stressed, wanting God's best for everyone impacted, but not able to steer the outcomes.

We met on a picture-perfect day of sun and snow in the mountains of Montana. I asked soul-depth questions and listened. Conversation flowed easily. After a few hours, I asked Steve to assess why, despite his decades of mature faith, generosity and success, he was so stressed and weighed down.

"I think it's because I'm still owning it," was his reply.

We talked for a while about Steve trusting God and desiring to surrender the future to Him. I looked for something tangible to help Steve mark his memory to create real change—real peace.

GIVING AWAY YOUR CAR . . . AND LIFE

"What would you do if you wanted to give away one of your cars?" I asked. *"You'd find the title deed, sign it over to the person you were giving it to, and then hand the deed over to them."*

We then began to imagine what a title deed to his life might look like—specifically, what he would list on it. We talked about what it would feel like to turn *every* aspect of his life over to God. In some ways it seemed scary, he admitted, but he knew those were just feelings based on lies of fear. When we then talked about what we'd both experienced in our decades of believing and following Christ, we were energized and fascinated by His love and kindness to us. Of course, we could trust Him—with everything.

It helped that we were having this conversation on a chairlift against the backdrop of the epic mountains and big sky. God's handiwork seemed like His signature, assuring us He is an impeccable owner who treasures *all* of His creation—be it a mountain range, a man's business, or his life.

On his flight home, Steve started writing a document he titled "Deed to My Life." He listed many things, including his mind, body, wife, marriage, daughter, his past, present and future, his business and its prospects, his wealth and possessions. The process helped him give ownership of his life and dilemmas over to God. He added some Bible verses to the document reminding himself of God's total trustworthiness. At the bottom, he wrote, *Whenever I start to stress, I will remember this deed.*

> Writing out the deed to my life reveals what I am grasping. It can help me transfer ownership of my life and dilemmas to God.

Circumstances and business details didn't flip into easy mode after the deed transfer, but Steve's demeanor and feelings changed dramatically. He told me his life had changed because his heart changed. His perspective, attitude, and peace were, and still are, significantly better.

Turns out, that encounter meant as much to me as for Steve. A few months later, I wrote out my own title deed. I listed everything I could think of: my family, relationships, enterprises, money, possessions, reputation, future, deepest longings, strengths, flaws, and nagging fears. Then, like Steve did with his, I transferred my deed over to Father God.

That ownership transfer pops into my mind often. Whenever I

> Remembering that my life's title deed has been given over to God opens my eyes to the lies of my ego and bankruptcy of my self-made operating system.

start generating ideas and future plans on my own—trying to own my future—remembering the title deed recalibrates my brain. It reminds me that God plans smarter and kinder than me. It helps me overcome the lie that I'm not enough and quenches my yearning for significance. Giving fears over to God takes them away as we ask God to show us the lies that cause them.

TURNING OVER OWNERSHIP

When we turn ownership over to our Father, He opens our eyes to aspects of ourselves that have been shaped by our past, our fears, and our flawed nature. God calls that nature our *flesh*—which is where our capacity for sin resides. God also shows us what our operating system has been, the schemes we've developed to try to make sure things go our way. But our self-made operating system only gives the illusion of control. It delivers no true satisfaction. It may seem to work for a while, muffling our fears and even producing external results that others envy, but it's not reliable. It doesn't last.

> Fear may be a fierce motivator, but it is a terrible master. It blinds me to what God wants to give me by His grace.

How would you describe your operating system? What do you do to try to get life running on your terms?

The problem with our self-designed operating systems is they're powered by fear—fear that we won't measure up, won't win, or won't be admired. Fear that we'll be rejected and won't be accepted or belong. Fear we won't be loved.

Fear is a tyrant. It's a fierce motivator, but a terrible master. Fear blinds us to what God wants to give us. It pivots us away from grace, away from love and truth from our Father. It blocks joy.

Fear and insecurity can only be truly overcome by transferring the ownership of our life over to God. We need perfect love to cast out fear.

To receive love, we must trust—and transfer ourselves into the hands and ownership of the One who is love.

What stops us from trusting God so we can go *all in* with Him? The short answer is—doubt (which is just fear in other clothes). We may doubt that God is everything He says He is or that He fully accepts us and will give us all that He has promised. We probably have plenty of doubts about what His plans are for us, too. We'd still like to script those ourselves.

> One expression of fear is doubt. Doubt holds me back from totally trusting God, and that causes me to settle for my own version of "good" outcomes.

Doubt holds us back from totally trusting God, and that causes us to settle for our own version of "good" outcomes. Sadly, these outcomes are incomplete and inferior. They're missing full perspective. They focus only on the here and now. They miss the long term and the eternal life that we can't yet see.

ALL IN MEANS LETTING GO

Turning ownership of our life over to God seems radical. It is, meaning it gets to the very root. It's going *all in* with His plans and purposes as better than our own. A major step toward this will be letting go of the past, particularly:

- lies about God, myself, or life—lies driving my fears
- shame over my failures and any disparaging self-talk I repeat to myself
- ego-inflating recognition and false feelings of superiority because of my accomplishments—especially those that have formed the basis of my identity
- disappointments and the offenses or sins others have committed against me
- bitter resentment, unforgiveness, and contempt

Letting God *own* you also means giving Him control of:

- your body and what you do with it
- your mouth and what you say
- your thoughts and where you let them take you

Guys, our perfect Father knows and wants the very best for us. He brought it to us in His Son. Jesus is the ultimate real and good man. He alone enables us to be our real self, and to be good (beneficial to others). Let's receive God's very best. Let's recapture His vision for manhood, which is being like Jesus. Let's receive and enjoy the gift of our identity in Jesus as sons of the Father. Let's invite Him to mold us as men.

Remember, manhood is a team sport. Now is the time to build and enjoy the teamwork of a few deep friends—*Level 5 Friends.*

Live the *Receive Principle*. It fuels everything. Receive Christ as your solution, your Savior, your Lord, your friend. Receive your identity and approval as your Father's son. Receive Jesus' righteousness, His purpose, His guidance, and His power. Live from that identity. Cancel the enemy's lies of shame. Receive full forgiveness, adoption and your perfect destiny in the Father's home and eternal kingdom.

> As a team sport, manhood involves living by receiving, by transforming, by huddling and by lifting others as we join in the Father's work.

Live to *Transform*. The purpose of your life is to become more like Jesus. God is the transformer. He improves. Welcome His lifelong transformation in you. Every day, in every situation, remember *LIFT*—Life Is For Transformation.

Huddle **regularly** (weekly works well) with a few real and deep friends. Make everything in your life visible to them so you gain self-awareness, perspective, and encouragement. You have nothing to fear and much to gain from being real and known.

Live to *Lift*. God lifts us. Join Him in lifting, encouraging and empowering others. Use whatever you have to improve situations and life for others. Lift up God by spreading the joy of Christ and glory of the Father.

Quit your struggle. Scrap your inadequate operating system. Surrender full ownership to the perfect owner. Receive Jesus fully. Receive His forgiveness fully. Forgive yourself, your dad or anyone else you've allowed to harden your heart. End your victimhood and bondage to bitterness. Run to the Father. Live as His son. Ask Him to Re-Father you. He'll guide you in every situation in all of life.

ASK MYSELF

* "What parts of my life am I holding on to with a tight grip? Realistically, what % of my life and future have I put into God's ownership?"

MY ACTIONS

* I will begin an honest conversation with God about who has the most beneficial intent and comprehensive control of my life—Him or me?
* I will stop striving to run my life. I will start taking the greatest steps, turning over ownership. The work to move me out of the way so God will work is prayer. Prayer is the greatest work because it invites God to work.

"If any of you wants to be my follower, you must give up your own way, take up your cross, and follow me. If you try to hang on to your life, you will lose it. But if you give up your life for my sake and for the sake of the Good News, you will save it. And what do you benefit if you gain the whole world but lose your own soul?" —Jesus in Mark 8:34-5 NLT

"There is only one type of life that truly wins and that is the one that places faith in the hands of the Savior. Until that is done, you are on an aimless course that goes nowhere."

—John Wooden

A CLOSING REMINDER

This manhood journey—and the healing and transformation you desire in your life—**is NOT ON YOU.**

It depends on God. He is the solution. He is the Way. He is the power. You just need to receive it. I'm living proof. I've been experiencing it.

I'm a visionary guy, prone to dream bigger than I can live up to. A spontaneous extrovert. Ideation is my strength; follow-through is my weakness. But God has been working in me.

Before you start on this journey, I want to give you a word of warning. Don't be shocked if your expectations rise but your confidence tanks as you start this journey over the next few weeks or months.

If you start to feel that way, know that I felt that exact way. It happened to me after I read a great book called *Unoffendable* by Brant Hanson a couple years ago with a few couples. My wife and everyone seemed to become less offendable, but I got worse. I got more thin-skinned, prickly, and defensive. Weird, huh?

I think God was showing me something crucial. Self-help is not the

> The manhood journey reveals the truth that ultimate answers are only received from God, not earned.

answer. I have more pride and more flaws than I realized. He was showing me that ultimate answers are only received from God, not earned.

It reminds me of my neighbor's generator. She asked me to start it for her in a big storm and power outage. After pulling the cord on my Briggs & Stratton generator to power our home, I ran across the street and up her driveway to see what I could do with her shiny electric key-start Honda Generator that wouldn't start.

> I need a power source greater than myself to fuel my life. His name is Jesus.

Ahhh. Dead battery. Oh, cool. A battery recharging plug in. Perfect. I'll plug an extension cord into it and run it into her garage to plug it in for recharging the battery.

So, I did, just before confidently (and idiotically!) turning the key, fully expecting the power to come through the cord and start the generator.

Not! I was in a powerless electrical death loop, and I missed the clues.

Moral of the story: I need a power source greater than myself to fuel my life.

My encouragement for you: Let Go. Let God. Surrender to and receive from Him.

Tell yourself, "Get out of God's way, so He can work in me way better than I can."

Remember this: Father God makes great things, and He made you. Receive what Jesus achieved for you. You are God's adopted son. He delights in you. You're on a team of brothers. You have what it takes. You have a purpose, and you matter. You're a good man!

ACKNOWLEDGMENTS

Huge thanks to:

MEN I INTERVIEWED—Ed Tandy McGlasson, Reese Butler, Michael Trover, Mark Merrill, Pat Lencioni, Tony Dungy, Robert Lewis, Paul Cole, Tony Bennett, Brian O'Connor, Brian Boland, Linda Obremski, Jack Grogger, Bob Shank, Rod Hairston, Miles McPherson, Doug Baldwin, Benjamin Watson, Russell Wilson, Shane Williamson, Ed Uszynski, Jim Daly, David Robbins, Gary Oliver, Ron Tijarina, Matt Haviland, Ray Roberts.

PEOPLE WHO ENDORSED THE BOOK AND THOSE WHO REVIEWED CHAPTERS—Thank you for caring, reading and investing in this cause with me.

HUDDLE FRIENDS—Greg Weaver and Pete McIndoe. John Blumberg, Johnny Parker, David Dusek and Kent Evans. Dave Chae. Jason Pederson and Mike Harbour.

SEATTLE HUDDLE FRIENDS AND GROUPS—Tom Flick, Jim Zorn, Mike Clark, Jerry Brown's C3 Leaders Group, Matt McIlwain and the Friday Bible Study Guys.

MENTORS/ADVISORS—Don Wallis, Clark Donnell, Tom Rhodes, Mike Mortier. Mike Woodruff. Les Parrott, Gary Thomas, Scott Sticksel, Rick Christian, Bob Lepine. Mike Gardner. Dennis Rainey. Mitch Temple. Kenny Luck.

CHAPLAINS & LEVEL 5 TEAMMATES—John Werhas, Chuck Obremski, Norm Evans, George Toles, Pat Richie, Jerry Mitchell, Charlie Marck, George Lilja, George Andrews, Jackie Slater, Mike Moroski, Eugene Robinson, Steve Largent, Paul Skansi, Kelly Stouffer, Reggie White.

LEGACY MEN—Dad, Chuck Obremski, Bill Walsh, Peb Jackson, BJ Weber.

MEN HUDDLE TEAM—Kent Evans, Hunter Mills, Jon McCallon, Ryan Sanders, Paul Fey, Chad Hodge.

MY EDITORS AND PUBLISHER—Tim Grissom for living this message and investing in men. I appreciate your excellence and perseverance in distilling my quantity into quality over the last 3-1/2 years. Paul Fey, thank you for being my strong clean-up batter on this book. Kent Evans, for your mission-minded excellence, execution, and persistent wisdom as my publisher and partner.

HOME TEAM—Mom for your encouragement and prayer. Kyle, Kory, Kolby, Keegan for our awesome experiences, joys, laughs, humbling lessons for me, support, prayers . . . and for being devoted to your families.

Stacy, thank you for encouragement, prayer, promptings of discipline and a life of love, wisdom and help. You complement all my gaps and my couple strengths. I still chuckle (and chafe, since I'm a rascal) at your big sigh when I finished this life-smothering project, telling me, "This is the last book you ever write!"

How about this? "We'll only do what God gives us to do."

Most essentially, Father God, Lord Jesus, Holy Spirit, thank You for pursuing, forgiving and adopting me. Thank You for re-Fathering me and offering Yourself and the way of Jesus to us all. All gratitude and glory go to You.

RECEIVE more with the *Field Guide*
Dive deeper with RECEIVE: The Way of Jesus for Men Field Guide

Positive change comes when we receive and experience more. Process this life-long message with a consistent and guided path. The FREE Field Guide helps you personalize and shape your own plan to progress.

It will help you:

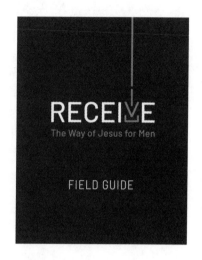

- Grow by connecting daily to Abba Father as His son
- Develop self-awareness, relationship goals and key habits
- Easily discuss with a friend or small group

Experience this to get closer to Abba Father and trusted friends as you discern how to become a better man.

Learn more at www.jeffkempteam.com/receive-field-guide

Level 5 Friendship Playbook
Start huddling and go deeper with the free playbook

Friendship is the way of Jesus! Life for guys gets way better with Level 5 Friendships that energize and protect your life. You can download it for free at www.menhuddle.com.

The *Level 5 Friendship Playbook* offers proven coaching, easy steps and reliable tips to get there. It gives you and your friends a starting point, clear vision, and coaching tips along the way.

- Download the free *Level 5 Friendship Playbook* (10-minute read)
- Get tips to find the right guys, ensure trust, and connect consistently
- Gain self-awareness weekly from the Self X-Ray
- Share with your men's group, church, or organization to increase friendship and brotherhood

If you want to spread Level 5 Friendship, email us at info@jeffkempteam.com to learn more about opportunities to connect and grow with other men.

Snag the playbook today at www.menhuddle.com!

Read and share *FACING THE BLITZ*
Three Strategies for Turning Trials into Triumphs

Develop the capacity to thrive, even when life hits hard. Just as dangerous blitzes create opportunity for a prepared quarterback and team, every trial is an opportunity to grow and advance. The courageous example of Jesus and stories from various leaders and the NFL give key coaching for relationships and leadership.

> "Full of wisdom, hope, and practical advice . . . easy to read, remember, and use."
>
> **—Pat Lencioni**

> "Solid, biblical advice for confronting life's most difficult challenges."
>
> **—Jim Daly**

> "This book will make a difference in your life. Read, digest, and reread it. Share it with friends to help them through difficulties and to strengthen their important teams, from family to business to sports."
>
> **—Tony Dungy**

The book provides reflection questions to help turn personal trials into triumphs. And you can pair it with the free *"Huddle Up" Group Discussion Guide* at www.FacingTheBlitz.com to be even more prepared!

Bring Jeff Kemp to Your Group
He can inspire in-person or virtually

Jeff's biggest impact comes through speaking live as he casts vision, unites teams, and models the way of Jesus. He engages audiences by **bringing his messages to life** with personal stories, humor, and heart-level transparency. People draw energy and LIFT from Jeff at:

- Men's events and retreats
- FamilyLife *Weekend to Remember* conferences
- Corporate leadership summits and team training sessions

Numerous CEOs have turned to Jeff for *Soul Coaching* which brings the various aspects of Jeff's message to an individualized and personalized coaching relationship.

Learn more at jeffkempteam.com/invite-jeff-to-speak

Manhood Journey Helps Dads Become Disciple-Makers
Are you a father who wants to intentionally disciple his children?

Manhood Journey resources can help.

If you're a father, you know that raising godly children is a difficult yet rewarding challenge. We can't do it alone, and we can't do it without God's power and blessing.

Manhood Journey exists to help dads become disciple-makers. We do this through a wide array of resources:

- Group and 1on1 Bible studies
- The *Father On Purpose* podcast
- *Mountain Monday* weekly newsletter
- Free eBooks, Reading Plans and more!

If you're a dad who wants to intentionally disciple your children, check out the Manhood Journey resources today.

Gear up at www.manhoodjourney.org

Other Resources from MJ Press
Christian books written to help dads, men and husbands thrive

MJ Press—the publishing arm of Manhood Journey—produces books that help men grow and thrive as fathers, husbands, and leaders. We are delighted to have partnered with Jeff Kemp on *Receive!* What a powerful message God has shared through him for us men.

If you'd like to read more on how to become a godly man, husband, or father, consider these other titles from MJ Press:

Bring Your Hammer
28 Tools Dads Can Grab from the Book of Nehemiah

More Than the Score
Cultivating Virtue in Youth Athletes

Wise Guys
Unlocking Hidden Wisdom from the Men Around You

www.manhoodjourney.org/mj-press

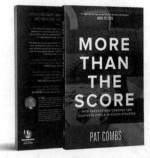